So You Think You Were Born

Poor

To our Good
friends from
th North
Giles & Betty

Richardson
&
Carol.

So You Think You Were Born

Poor

Wayne Richardson

To order additional copies of this book, contact:
Xlibris Corporation
1-888-795-4274
www.Xlibris.com
Orders@Xlibris.com
61299

CONTENTS

I thank my wife Carol for her help and for editing this book.

FOREWORD

I have often thought that I would like to document some of my life and experiences since I have lived in some people's minds what might be considered some rather interesting times.

Being born about as poor as any church mouse in the nation, I somehow survived and went on to enjoy a pretty good life. Being the youngest of eight kids, I was spoiled, so they tell me, by my older sisters, but we all survived to a ripe old age.

I started writing my memoirs in 1997 then left it sit until now which is 2007. I guess what prompted me to get motivated was the fact that at Christmas of 2006, I had to have spinal surgery and then in May of 07 I had knee surgery and two days later I had a mild stroke. By stroke standards it was mild, but it was an awakening call to let me know how close I was to the end, when all of a sudden I couldn't see very well, staggered when I walked and could not sign my name so it was legible. My dear wife Carol got me to the hospital stat where they kept me for three days. After six weeks, I was almost back to normal but a lot weaker.

I now have come to the conclusion I better get off my duff and finish this while I still have a few of my senses left..

I spent two years in the Navy, eight years with the Milwaukee Railroad, five years with the Montana Power Company and along with five years of night school, I gained enough experience to be called to work overseas for the U.S.Government

I thank my wife Carol for her help and for editing this book.

CHAPTER 1

MOM AND DAD

*M*y Father, John S Richardson, born on October 27, 1883 was the son of Joseph and Nancy Richardson from Faubush, Kentucky. My Mother, Electa Garner, born on February 14, 1887 was the daughter of George & Maffie Garner.

John and Electa were married in September of 1906 in Somerset, Kentucky and they farmed on Grandmother Richardson's farm near Faubush. Oscar Garner, my Mother's brother was living in Montana and convinced them that this was the new frontier and they should come. In 1910 they packed up with two small babies and ended up on a farm near Three Forks. There Dad and Oscar farmed together for about three years, but Dad couldn't get along with Oscar so Oscar Garner went down by Dillon and farmed there until he later returned to Kentucky. Dad then leased a place in what was known as the Dry Hills south of Manhattan from E.J. Parkins. There they prospered and in 1918 dad even bought a brand new 1918 Buick. He got a burr under his saddle and left after seven years and took on a Sharecrop farm owned by Doc Smith near Central Park . By this time they had five daughters and while at the Smith Ranch, Joe was born. They then left and went to the Chris Dauter's place and stayed three years. The big earthquake hit there in 1925 and Dad got another wild hair and went back to Kentucky. They stayed for about two years and starved but managed to get enough money for train fare back to Montana.

Dad and mom lived through some mighty hard times and as a result we as kids had to share them. Dad was not the most astute business person so as a result we spent most of our years growing up as share-croppers on different farms. After a few years and now with four daughters they starved out and moved back to Montana where they stayed.

My oldest sister, Fair, had married an immigrant German and they lived in Three Forks, Montana near the headwaters of the Missouri River. We moved in with them and by now mom and dad had eight kids counting Fair, now married to John Rempp and they had a daughter Charlotte who happened to be two months older than I. I was born while we lived there and without any money to buy baby stuff. John, who worked part time in a meat market, brought home a box that they used for shipping fish and that became my bassinet. So after dad and mom moved out of their cabins and rented a farm, we all ended up in the place that dad rented. Charlotte my niece and I pretty much grew up together.

Wedding picture, John Richardson
and Electa Garner   Sept.1906

CHAPTER 2

ALL THE KIDS

Fair

*B*y this time the oldest daughter Fair was 19 and she wanted to get out and do anything better than they had. Dad would not let his girls date a young man because he just wasn't going to have his girls gettin in the "Family Way". She married John Rempp, a German immigrant who was a stowaway on a ship coming over and they lived in a log cabin on a small farm near Three Forks. According to Fair when we visited her in 1998 when she was 90 years old, she had married John so they could get out of Kentucky. She said she did it for the kids because they were going hungry and living conditions were so bad. When they first arrived from Kentucky Dad and the family moved in with them I think they must have lived there only a year or two. John was a butcher and was one of the best because he had gone through his apprenticeship in Germany as a young man. He was a lousy farmer and a lazy one but a good butcher. In Germany every young man had to learn a trade. If his scholastic grades were not at a certain level at the end of his eighth year of school, he could not go on to high school or to college. He then must enter a trade apprenticeship and would be assigned to a firm for very little money and strict discipline. By the time he completed his apprenticeship of perhaps four years, John was a journeyman craftsman.

Oldest to the youngest, left to the right
Fair—Alma—Vivian—Leva—Ruth—Joe— Carol — Wayne

Joe & Wayne
1945 ?

Carol's 1st fish
Flathead 2004
8 lb trout

Biking from
Mesa Regal, AZ
1996

Snowmobiling
Kelly,Ryan,Jordan
Wayne 2006

Carol with our
Boxer Lonnie
2005

Out on the Lake
2003

The cabins we lived in near 3 Forks,MT. There were 8 of us kids + Mom & Dad +
John and the oldest sister Fair and their kid. The main 2 room log house
has been torn down. The barn and 2 cabins remain. My bassinet was a
wooden box that fish had been shipped to the 3 Forks meat market.
My sister Carol & I and present owner are in photo.

From left to right: Sister Elma, son Douglas, Carol,
Mother, Wayne and dad

Wayne, 3 years old and Carol, 6 years old

Alma

Around this time Alma, the second oldest sister, married Warren Grim who was a mail clerk on the Milwaukee Railroad. In those days they would pick up mail on the run in rural areas with an arm extended from the mail car, which was always the first or second coach behind the engine. The mail clerks in the mail car then sorted the mail and would drop it off as required and or reroute it when they came to larger towns. It was a mobile Post Office so to speak. He was much older than Alma but he made excellent money and I think she was bound and determined not to live her life in poverty. In 1940 they divorced and it was the usual bickering. Warren was going to take Doug away from her and she was determined to keep him. The courts eventually gave her custody. Doug lives in Missoula and has three children.

She then married Kenneth Dennis who also worked for the Milwaukee Road as a secretary to the Division Superintendent. Most of the family wasn't so sure that she made the best decision because Kenneth was a skinflint in some ways. He was commissioned as a Lieutenant and went into the army shortly after they married. He was sent to India where he spent the entire duration running a railroad battalion. He would send home part of his check every month and he instructed her to invest it into IBM stock most of the time. She was working for The Grand Silver Dime Store for the whole time he was in the service. I am not sure but her monthly pay was about $75 a month with $25 a month for rent. I know she had to really scrimp to make ends meet.

After the war Kenneth went back to work for the Milwaukee as the secretary to the Division Manager where he worked for the rest of his working career. Later he bought the apartment house at 21 North Jackson Street where they had been living in one of the ground floor apartments. Kenneth wouldn't spend a nickel until the buffalo pooped a little, if they went out to lunch for hamburgers. When they got home he would enter the cost of the lunch in his expense log, plus any tip that was paid. However when they retired they would spend their winters in Las Vegas and the summers in Deer Lodge, Montana. I would make a pilgrimage to visit them about once a season since I now lived in San Diego where I had started Nordic Refrigeration. Ken and Alma would make sure that we went to see one of the good Casino shows with dinner included and he never let you pick up the check. When I would depart back to San Diego he would always slip a $100 dollar bill in my pocket.

Kenneth died in 1989. He was walking down to the Post Office in Las Vegas to pick up his daily mail and as he stepped off the sidewalk to cross the street. He stepped on an oily spot where the taxis had parked he slipped, fell and hit his head on the pavement. He was taken to the hospital where he died a few days later of a brain hemorrhage. I believe he was about 81 years old.

Alma commuted back and forth to winter in Las Vegas and summer in Deer Lodge, Montana with her son, Paul.

And later Joe, her brother found her an apartment in Anaconda and moved her and Paul up there from Deer Lodge. A few years later she came down with shingles and to this day, 2002, she has suffered with them which has been around 10 years. Years ago she also developed glaucoma and is nearly blind. When she first contacted them, she didn't go to the doctor for about four days and he diagnosed her condition as shingles. He recommended pills which cost $10.00 a pill and she asked him what the alternative was. He told her she could take Tylenol and she elected to save the money.

At this time she was worth probably 20 million dollars. Kenneth and she had been transferring the bulk of their estate to Paul, who was in Havre working as a pharmacist. He couldn't come home so, Jean and Joe took care of her for the summer. She had big water blisters on her body and she was in terrible pain.

Paul was born in 1939 and he has never married probably because for the last ten years of her life he took care of her.

Vivian

The third daughter was born in Kentucky March 23, 1913.

As the girls grew up and having no boys in the family to help Dad in the fields, they had to take over and learn to harness horses and how to handle them. When we lived on the farm east of Manhattan, Montana, they were in the fields every day working right with Dad. I remember one time we had a loco horse named Barney. He was like a person who had used LSD; he would go along for awhile and work just fine, then he would go wild and you could hardly hold him. Dad was short of horses so Vivian said, "Give me that son-of-a-bitch, I'll work him." She was the Calamity Jane of our family. She was tough and she worked him part of a day before he had a flash-back and he reared up, kicked, broke the tongue, tore up the harness and she had a run-a-way on her hands. I was young then and I don't remember whether Dad ran to stop him or Vivian did, anyway nobody got injured or killed. A few days later Dad found a man that said he would take him off his hands and so we went to deliver him a few miles away. Vivian was sitting in the back seat of the old 1919 Dodge with the rope coming in the rear side window and they had gone about a mile when old Barney reared up and went crazy. Vivian had made the mistake of having the halter rope looped around her hand and when he jerked back, she couldn't let go and the rope cleaned off a lot of skin from her hand. Dad got out and caught old Barney and brought him up to the car. He then tied him to the spare tire holder on the back of the car. When he got in he said, "You Son-of-a-bitch you will run the rest of the way or I'll drag you". He made that horse run or trot the next mile or so till we got him delivered. Mom tore off a piece of a petticoat and wrapped Vivian's hand and when we got home we did our own first aid. Today we would have run to the emergency room of the nearest hospital. Doc Stanchfield was our Doc Adams of Gunsmoke and he did make house calls. I know today she doesn't have a scar that I recall.

During this time, after they got through in the fields at night they would come in around 6:00PM, unharness the horses, feed them, get the cows in, feed them and get a few hogs fed, then milk the cows, crank up the hand separator and run all the milk through to separate the cream from the milk. Then you could eat supper around 8:00 PM or later. 5:00 AM the next morning you were at it again.

As of 2003 all eight of us kids are still living. In 1998 my wife, Carol, and I visited my oldest sister, Fair, in Minneapolis and she admitted that if Dad hadn't worked the girls like mules we wouldn't all be around today. She is 95 now and I am the youngest and we are all still living.

Vivian didn't get married until she was close to 40 years old. She married Fred Coombs, an engineer on the Milwaukee Railroad and remained with him until his death in the 90's. Shingles finally got him and I think the pain was so intense that it eventually drove him crazy in the end. The shingles settled in his eye and I know there is nothing more tender that a person's eye and nothing, in my opinion, is more painful than shingles. I know because I had a mild case of them which settled in my left shoulder and arm and the pain is excruciating. Thank God for my wife Carol, because as soon as the pain started in my shoulder, she insisted that I go to the doctor. Mine only lasted a little over a month and there still is a little residual pain in the shoulder at night. When Fred was younger he was a fastidious dresser. He was part English and part Indian and I guess he got his fine clothes habit from the English. Even if he was going to the store for a small order of groceries he would put on his suit, top coat if the weather was cool and his homburg hat. Vivian liked that and so she also dressed very nicely.

Leva

The fourth girl to come into the family was born on March 27, 1915 and still no son. I guess Dad was pretty disappointed but what could he do. I think he disliked Leva from the start because she wasn't a boy. All the while she was growing up he called her Mutt and at times when the girls couldn't perform as well as a boy, he would lose his temper and whip them terribly. Today he would have landed in jail for child abuse.

Leva worked for J. C. Penney Co. in Bozeman for around 20 years and she managed the ladies departments of the store. She took care of the reordering of stock and the manager of the store had very little to do in assisting her. She was paid $2.10 per hour and the man that managed the men's department was paid $3.25 per hour and he couldn't even take care of the ordering for his department. Leva was an easy going person and didn't want to make waves so she would not complain.

Leva has two kids both living in Bozeman and they check on her daily to keep her little pellet stove loaded and that she is OK.

Ruth

The fifth girl to come along was Ruth, December 8, 1918. About all I can say about her is that she and I were 3 kids apart. I know all the girls helped Mom in caring for me. All the girls had a very hard life and they all worked in the fields when needed. However Ruth was somewhat the lazy one of the family and would duck any work that she could. She wouldn't admit it in her older years but her sisters claim that she would climb up to the top of a big cottonwood tree and hide so she wouldn't have to help with the dishes. All the girls except Carol had to help milk cows and do outside chores.

Ruth had married Russel Robinette after the war and he was a heavy drinker when he could get it. After I got out of the Navy I bought 1936 Chrysler coupe for $250. And it was a good running car. Russ borrowed it one day to go to Three Forks, 35 miles away to supposedly get a job. He got drunk and coming home he probably had it floor boarded when he came the approach at the Madison River Bridge, hit the heavy cable guard and flipped the car. That cable put a crease right down through the roof about six inches deep but lucky Russ didn't get a scratch. I lost one good car.

That marriage didn't last two long and Russ went from bad to worse and he ended up in a drug hospital. He died in his 50's as far as I know. Ruth married Burt Imeson after that and they had two more kids. Ruth died in 2005 at age 87. Burt was a heavy smoker and he died in a VA hospital of throat cancer after Ruth's death.

Joe

Finally, Dad got his son that he so much wanted all his life but as Joe grew older he became a little head strong and he and Dad did not get along too well. In fact by the time Joe was 16 he hated Dad. At 18 he left home with Joe LaBree who lived at the Poor Farm across the road from us at Townsend. They headed south for Arizona and the old Model a Ford broke down in Tremonton, Utah. They managed to get a little money together for repairs with money brother Joe made working for a rancher, Clinton Allen. Joe LaBree wanted to keep going south to Arizona but Brother Joe wanted to stay because he figured he had a job and a roof over his head so Joe LaBree left alone. He made it to Arizona but died shortly afterward. Brother Joe is gone now. I think I covered this somewhere else.

Carol

At this writing Carol is widowed, lives alone in Bozeman and her house is just two blocks from Leva and they see each other daily. All my sisters keep their homes neat as a pin. Her two children, Sharon and Dick both live in Bozeman and they make sure she is well taken care of. All of my sisters never let themselves get fat and they still look trim and fit and their hair is always nicely done. All of my sisters aged very well and were mentally sharp up till the last year or so of their life.

I, Wayne covered my history as the author of this book.

When we lived on the Weaver ranch east of Manhattan with eight kids, John and Fair lived with us and their daughter Charlotte. We had mattresses on the floor to accommodate everyone and the few beds that we had, usually three kids slept together. I slept between Mom and Dad until I was about six years old, and mind you, they did not have queen or king sized beds in those days. I remember Alma came over one time and she pulled up the mattress off the floor that we had been sleeping on and it was frozen to the floor. I think they went to the straw stack and brought some straw in to put under it.

Wayne

And then last came Wayne, the author which is covered in many parts In those days it was sleep with Mom and Dad or freeze with the older kids in the winter which I did from the time I was seven on. I really don't know why we didn't die because we were all skinny as a rail and we didn't have the warm clothes that we do today.

I am the youngest of eight children and my mother was 41 years old when I was born while we lived with John and Fair in the log cabin not very far from the headwaters of the Missouri River. As late as 2002 the cabin was still standing and I drove by it many times through the years. The main house burned down sometime in the past and a new frame house was built in that spot. As of 2006 the two single room log cabins are still standing but the one used as the wash house is in pretty bad shape, however the other one used as sleeping quarters for the girls has had the old sod roof removed and replaced with a gabled roof and steel paneling.

My older sisters tell me that in the rainy season the sod roofs would leak and they would set pans on the bed where it would drip through. When they wanted to turn over they would carefully lift the pans, pour the water in a bucket, turn over, then replace the pans. As of 2005 all four of my older sisters, ranging in age from 91 to 98 were still alive.

The barn is still in relatively good condition and in all of these buildings you can see the marks on the wood indicating that the logs were hued with a broad ax by a man with good skills.

In 1928 women went through the menopause in their early 40's at that time. Now in the 90's it is not uncommon, so I have been told, for women to be in their late 50's before they enter this period.

Anyway, I guess only the older girls knew that Mother was pregnant till she was about to deliver, and on February 25, 1928 she did just that and brought forth the last of her family that she would bare. I was 25 inches long and Doc Smith said that was the longest baby he had ever delivered. I was born in the Bozeman Deaconess Hospital and was so weak that none of the family thought I would survive. I was born with rickets and was fed orange juice when they could get it and other good foods of the time. They didn't have a bassinet for me to sleep in so John brought home a wooden fish box that fish had been shipped in to the Three Forks Meat Market and that became my bassinet. I was nearly a year old before I got enough strength to hold my head up off my shoulders, so my sisters told me. Around this time a rat got into my crib at night and had chewed off the end of my ring finger, left hand. My crying woke my mother and she got up and ran the rat off and she was so frightened because there was blood all over me. As it turn out it wasn't so bad. My finger nail is a little uneven but unless you were told you could not see it today. At around two years of age I was able to start walking and from then on I was on my way. Oh, I would never become a brain surgeon or a rocket scientist but I had reasonable intelligence and went on to make a place in this world for myself.

I later ran into Doc when we were both by chance having lunch at the Oak Bar and Grill in Bozeman. He was around 90 years old and he still went to his office every day. He bragged to me that he could still tie knots with the best of them yet today, referring to sutures. He remembered our family and asked how they were and remembered them by name. I was working for Lovelace Motor in the shipping and stocking department while still going to high school at that time. We moved from John and Fair's in the Spring of '28 to a farm up on the Madison River area out of Three Forks, Montana where Dad worked for three years on the Adams Ranch. Around this time Alma the second oldest sister married Warren Grimm.

Fair, the olest died at at 99 in 2006
Alam died at 96 in 2006
Vivian died at 95 in 2008
Ruth died at 87 in 2005
Joe died at 83 in 2005
All that is left is Leva at 94, Carol at 84 and Wayne at 81 years old.

CHAPTER 3

MANHATTAN

*W*e then moved to a farm three and one-half miles east of Manhattan, Montana out on Dry Creek Road. This 160 acre farm was owned by a man named Weaver and we paid the usual rent for those days. Half of the hay grown and one-third of the grain was sold and went to the landlord. We had a garage, a barn, a chicken house and an outhouse. The house had no insulation in the walls and of course double pane windows were unheard of. The bedrooms where the kids slept had no heat and when we would go to bed in the winter we would take hot water bottles to warm the bed. In the mornings when it was extremely cold like 30 or 40 below, the hot water bottle would be frozen at the foot of the bed. Why we didn't die of pneumonia or something else I will never know. I do know that with eight kids living there someone always had a cold.

Alma, my older sister, gave me my first football for Christmas when I was about 7 years old and you cannot believe how happy I was with that. When weather warmed up in the spring I would carry it to school everyday. Warren, Alma's husband, loved to hunt pheasants and they came over regularly after we moved to the farm east of Manhattan. He would use a 12 gauge shotgun and Dad would hunt with his 32 S&W pistol. Dad would shoot the birds on the ground before they got airborne and many times he would shoot their heads off while Warren would get them in the air.

Later John and Fair moved in with us along with their daughter Charlotte who was two months older than I. We all lived in that house.

Adam Hefner and his brother who owned the Chicago Stock Yards at that time were in Montana visiting and they learned of our plight.

When they got back to Chicago they shipped us a complete house full of furniture that they had changed out of their house, all heavy solid Oak of good quality. We lived there for eight years.

As kids we had a happy time. The Hickel family lived across the road about one-third mile away and they had five kids. We played "Hide and go Seek" together many times in the evenings, gopher hunting with sling shots, swimming in the Bulls-Run Creek that went by the house and ice skating in the winter.

The Hickel family moved in about 1934 or 5 and the Tudor family moved onto the farm after that. They had just one boy with fiery red hair. Everett was about a year older than I so we played together. We would pull corn silk tassels off the corn, dry them and smoke them in corn cob pipes that we would make. We would take the butt end of a corn cob, dry it and remove the center, then take our pocket knives and drill a hole in the lower part, then insert a hollowed out sweet clover stem and voila (!), a corn-cob pipe. We then would smoke dried corn silks, dried dock-weed etc.; they all tasted terrible. Everette, lived across the road which was about a 1/4 mile from us. He would come over daily in the summer and he and I kept our pipes hidden behind a rock by the granary until one day Dad found them. We had our initials carved into the stem so Dad brought mine to the house and filled it with peerless chewing tobacco and handed it to me to smoke and insisted that I smoke some good tobacco. He took his pipe and we lit up together and during our little social time, he kept asking me how I felt and he just knew I was going to get sick. I didn't and he never mentioned smoking again.

By the time I was eleven we had graduated to Bull Durham which cost five cents and at 16 we smoked tailor-mades. For you younger folks Bull Durham was a roll-your-own and tailor-mades were factory made cigarettes as we know them today. When I was 21 I decided that smoking was like a baby sucking his thumb as a pacifier. I would crave for a cigarette when I would have a cup of coffee or after a meal and I was getting hooked on nicotine. I decided to quit and so I did, but at these times and within six months I found that a tooth pick substituted as my pacifier. I quit smoking and am smoke free today.

Our neighbors about two miles up the road from our farm had a bitch that littered out and they gave Joe a little puppy, half collie and half Australian shepherd. It was in January and around 20 below when one evening after chores, Joe and I walked up to get the dog. Talk about a cold walk. Joe stuffed the puppy inside his coat to keep him warm till we got home. We made him a bed in a cardboard box and kept him by the bed. At first he would get so cold we would sneak him in bed with us.

When I was seven or eight years old someone gave me a young kid Billy goat. I adopted it, bottle feeding it till it could eat on its own. I had a little red wagon and I taught the dog and goat to pull the red wagon with me in it. Then I would put them in it and let them ride.

At first the dog or goat would immediately jump out but after a few times they would stay in and ride. Later when I would have them pulling me they would get tired and would turn around and try to get in the wagon. I then would have to put one of them in the wagon and I would pull them. There wasn't room for both of them in the wagon so one would jump in the wagon and knock the other one out. I generally would divide the time that I would pull each of them. I remember one night it was 40 below zero and the dog and goat slept together in a dog house on the front porch with blankets to keep them warm. In the middle of the night the dog was barking and wouldn't shut up, we went out to check on them and the dog was mad as hell at the goat. It seems the goat, which we called Billy, had peed in the bed because it was too cold for him to get out of bed to go pee. We took the wet blankets out of their bed and got some dry ones from our rag bin, made them a clean bed and they went back to sleep. They ran and played together for a couple of years and believe me no one dared harm that goat or they had to do battle with Shep. One day, they had wandered off down by the Hespin farm a mile away from home which was next to the farm where the Payne boys lived. They were along the railroad track and Bud Payne saw them and killed the goat. I cried for days and finally Dad and I found him near the tracks down by the Pane farm. I suppose 20 years later I asked Bud Payne why he killed him and he said he didn't know they just did it. I wanted to deck him yet after all that time.

The Hespin family lived near the county road known as the Four Corners about one mile away. Joe was about 13 years old by this time and Bertha Hespin was about 14 or 15 and she had a crush on Joe. It was January of '35 and She had invited the Hickelsa, Richardson's and all to go ice skating on a slew by the farm. My dad had forbidden us kids to go but we went anyway. It was one mile away, 20 below zero and about eight inches of snow. Freddie and Johnny Hickel turned back and went home when the going got too tough. I didn't see them turn back and I kept toddling along.

We got down to the pond and built a fire and had put on our clamp on skates and were starting to have fun when our dad popped over the bank and was he angry! He ordered us off the ice immediately and we all started home at his pace and no matter how winded I got he didn't offer to help.

When we got home Mother and a couple of the older girls had baked bread and we all gathered around the kitchen stove to thaw out and have some hot bread and butter fresh out of the oven.

That night at about 2:00 AM I began to croup up and I was having trouble getting any air into my lungs. Dad got up, built up a fire and started the tea kettle. Mom put some Vicks or some other inhalant in the water and I was trying to breath in the steam. I was still having trouble so they got on the party line crank phone to call Doc. Stanchfield in Manhattan. He was a good family doctor. He got up and drove out the three and one-half miles on a dirt and snowy road to the farm. He gave Mom and Dad some strong stuff for me to breathe through the brown paper bag and I got a little better. He then showed Dad how to do a tracheotomy and left him a couple of surgical tools and a rubber hose. He told Dad that next time he came to town to drop them off at his office. Dad didn't have to use the knife but I had frosted my lungs and I had to stay home for six weeks until they healed. To this day I do not have the lung power that I should have. My teacher, Miss Aiken sent home school work with my sisters and I was home taught by one sister or another. I was able to go on to the second grade the next fall. I had mostly all "A's" in the second grade under Miss Hansen. Miss Hansen had large pop eyes and when she would get angry I swear it seemed like they were going to fall out. She was a good teacher in my mind but she had a terrible temper.

In the summer time we took wagon hub rims from an old junker wagon and would nail a stick to the end forming a "T" and would run all over the farm pushing this ring to keep it rolling. Every boy in those days carried a slingshot and we were deadly with them. Gophers or birds were just not safe if they were within range. During this time the State had a bounty on crows and magpies and we got a penny a pair for the feet from a young bird and three cents for an adult pair. We would string them up on a string and sometimes we might have 100 to 150 pairs to turn in. My ancestry came from Kentucky and I never knew that I wasn't supposed to refer to a slingshot as a nigger flip until I was 18 and in the Navy. I guess in the slave days they would use peas to flip the workers if they got lazy in the fields.

The winter of '35 and '36 was a bitch; we had deep snow and cold more than usual. The school bus route ran from Manhattan to Manard 17 miles one way. The road was all gravel so it was slow and rough. A few times we had gotten to school and within an hour they would announce that all kids riding the Dry Creek route were to report to their bus and were going back home because a blizzard was coming in. The teachers hurried and got us some home work to do and we left. Sometimes we just got a day off.

The bus was a 1934 Dodge and the only heater in those days was the one under the dash up front and was about the size of a toaster slice toaster, which wouldn't even keep the driver warm. Our driver for a number of years was Bud Burns and he was a happy go lucky guy who was always laughing. He also could maintain control and he had on occasions threatened to put a kid off the bus. I have seen him grab a high school kid and drag him off the bus. He never hit one but he did shape them up a time or two.

In January of 1936, it got to about 65 below zero. Our thermometer only went to 60 below but it was down in the bulb and I think the official temperature was around—65. We had some of Roy Harrison's horses boarded there and they would chase all the cows away from the straw stack. One of the cows broke through the fence in front of the chicken house and the next morning she had gone down to her knees with her nose resting on the ground, frozen solid. We kept the milking cows in the barn but it wasn't large enough to put all of the dry cows inside. Mind you, we lived in an old frame house with no insulation in the walls and if you didn't keep a fire going the inside temperature would almost match the outside temperature or so it felt. More than once the hot water bottle that you took to bed to warm your feet would be frozen the next morning.

In those days we had somewhat of a co-op telephone system. If the phone lines needed maintenance some of the men would have to go out and do it because the owner of the system might be busy somewhere else.. One long ring would get you the central operator if you wanted to call beyond Manhattan but if you wanted to call one of your neighbors on this line you rang direct. There was a wooden phone box on the wall that housed the phone and batteries and we had to replace them periodically. I still remember our number was 064F23. That meant for a neighbor to call us they had to crank two longs and three short rings.

Conference calls are nothing new. Sometimes so many people would pick up their receivers to "RUBBER IN" that the signal would get so weak that you would have to ask some of the people to hang up. You never knew who they were but we knew most of the time who the nosy bodies were. You knew who had a canary or the sound of certain dogs bark. The cost for this service was $1.00 per month.

Poor Leva was so embarrassed one morning; she wore an old pair of men's shoes to milk in and do the outside chores. They were dirty and had cow manure on them and she had forgotten to change shoes before school. She went to step into the bus and saw what had happened. Bud Burns was kind and he waited while Leva ran the 200 yards back to the house to change. The bus may have been a few minutes late for school but their schedule usually got us there about 15 minutes before the school bell would ring. The school bells in those days were big bronze bells and the janitors rang them to call classes to order. We didn't have the cheap ding ding type that they have today; we had class.

Manhattan schools were one of the best. We had good teachers and even though the buildings were old, we as kids didn't tear them up or mark them with graffiti. We knew that it was against the rules and didn't want to get a paddle across the butt if we did something wrong.

The grade school and the high school were within a hundred yards of each other and all the playgrounds were nice bluegrass lawns. Even the elementary playgrounds were lawns. We did have one dirt area on the south side where they loaded heating coal into a big concrete bunker and there is where we played marbles. We played with our toy trucks under some large pine trees digging up the loose dirt and building roads, but we outgrew that by about the third grade.

We had our little jack-asses also. Earl McLees used to tantalize me after school and would take a stick and whip me with it. He was two grades ahead of me and I was no fighter so he delighted in tantalizing me. While I was in the second grade, he convinced Gerald Roth that he could whip me and kept prodding him till we fought each other. I landed a lucky punch to his eye and won that round. Mr. Gas, our grade school principal gave him a good paddling for that but then he threatened to catch me off the school grounds and really beat me up. I had another minor fight with George De-Hon. I think we were fighting over the rules in playing marbles but it didn't amount to much. That about concludes all the fights I had till I got into high school in Bozeman. In my railroading days I will cover some more of the McLees fiasco.

My brother Joe was a favorite of Mother and I was favored by my father. Mother seldom ever swore but she had some odd thoughts. When she went through the menopause change she developed a hatred for Dad. I guess her mind must have snapped to a degree. She could never say anything complimentary about him and because he favored me she developed a negative attitude toward me. She tried to convince us kids that Dad was going to kill us. She firmly believed that Dad was going to poison us all. One time she took Joe to the garage where we kept our flour swung on a platform from the ceiling and there she showed Joe where someone had cut a corner of a 100 pound sack of flour and had put Paris green in it. She claimed Dad had done it and of course we all saw it. We got the sack down and scooped out enough flour to make sure all the Paris green was out and took it to the house to use. Paris green is a grass green powder that is used in the garden to keep insects off. It is poison but if you wanted to kill someone you certainly wouldn't use something as obvious as a green insecticide.

Mother also used to tell me on numerous occasions that Joe would grow up and amount to something but I was nothin' but Daddy's little Candy Pecker and would never amount to nothin'. I heard this many times in the eight years we lived on the Weaver farm. Mom was close to all her girls and they all worked hard as kids.

The girls and Mom washed clothes once a week and this was an all day job. They heated water in a big copper boiler on the stove and then poured it into a half drum like washer along with a partial cake of sliced up lye soap. We made our own soap in those days from the fat from the hogs we butchered. The scrubber part was also a half circle type unit that fit on arms that were pulled back and lowered into the washer drum on top of the clothes. For twenty minutes you rocked the scrubber back and forth over the clothes. With a hand ringer mounted on the side of the washer you wrung out the clothes and they fell into another tub of water where you rinsed them. The ringer was then swung a ¼ turn and you wrung out the clothes into a second rinse tub. From there they got their final rinse and ringing out and were hung on the clothes line to dry. I can remember a few times when I only had one pair of bib overalls and I had to run around in my underwear till they got dry. Saturday was generally wash day while all the girls were home from school to help. In the winter time they would freeze on the line and if you weren't careful when you removed them they would break into right where they hung over the wire and then you had rags or a repair job. We had an Aladdin lamp and several wick lamps for the house and we had a gas iron to press the clothes. We also had several sad irons that you heated on the stove then snapped a handle on them to iron clothes. The girls got lots of minor burns from these darn things.

In the Fall, we always butchered about four or five hogs and this became our winter's meat. Pork could be salt cured but beef was not so easy to preserve. We did can some beef but most of our diet was salt pork. It also was cured and stacked on wire hung racks either in the garage or root cellar. As I recall it did better in the dry air of the garage because it would mold in the dampness of the cellar.

I also remember how Dad was so ill tempered in this era. He never whipped me but twice and not really hard then. Once I did something wrong when I was about six or seven years old and he gave me a couple of light swats. I stepped away and said, "Ha Ha it didn't even hurt". He grabbed me back and when he got through I knew I'd had a lickin'.

For the older kids he used a piece of harness tug and I would cringe and feel so sorry for them. He beat them so hard and would leave cuts on their backs. It seemed that Dad took most his rage out on Leva. Joe, Ruth and Vivian got more than their share also. Carol and I being the youngest probably didn't get near the whippings that the older kids did. I tried to understand Dad as there were six or seven kids home at once and we were fighting fools. When something went wrong we thought nothing of slugging the opponent. If Dad got wind of it there was a whipping coming.

I remember one time Joe and Leva got into an argument about whose turn it was to turn the cream separator. Each claimed they had done it last and it was the others turn. Leva hauled off and slugged Joe in the nose and the blood flew. At about the same time we had a sorrel mare named Liz that had been sick with a bowel block and we had been walking her for over 24 hours. At that moment Ruth had been walking her when the mare broke loose and ran to the yard fence. She reared into the air several times nickering to get our attention. We all ran outside and once we were all there she turned and on a dead run took off for the lower pasture where the animal bone yard was. We all ran as fast as possible and when we got there, she was lying on a little knoll close to the bone yard, dead.

She was Dad's best mare. He then cranked up the old 1919 Dodge with a California top and called Doc Stanchfield to have him meet them at the office. With Joe's nose laying off to one side it was obvious that it was broken. Doc set the nose and he asked Dad how it happened. Dad related how a mare had died and Leva had slugged Joe. Dad asked how much he owed him and Doc said he couldn't believe a frail little girl could have done that and he said, "John, next time you come to town, bring that girl in because I can't believe she could have done it". Next week Dad made Leva go with them to town. She was so embarrassed when she walked into Doc's office; he looked at her and said, "It's hard to believe a skinny little girl like that could have done that John, but your bill is paid". Now at this age in our lives we can understand a little bit why Dad was the way he was. Vivian went by her first name Easter at that time because she was born on Easter Sunday.

She hated that name and after she left home she let people know that her name was Vivian which was her middle name. She was a tough gal; she could handle the toughest of horses. Easter was a worker and she worked right with the men in the fields during haying and threshing times. In fact all the older girls worked the same. Ruth and Carol had it a little easier than the four older girls.

Now mind you what Mother had instilled in our young minds about Dad trying to kill us, then bear in mind, the severe whippings he gave the kids and now the next episode. Leva was another girl who worked extremely hard but she had a milder temperament than Vivian. We had lots of rattlesnakes in this area and it was during haying time. Dad always carried a little 32 S&W pistol in his hip pocket of his overalls. Leva's job was driving the stacker team which hoisted the hay upon the stack. The hours were long and kids would grab a few winks whenever possible so between loads of hay sometimes you might have 20 minutes between loads. Dad had finished placing the hay on the stack and had come down to get a drink of water. There, lying in the shade of the stack was Leva asleep and stretched out beside her was a big rattlesnake within a foot of her head. Dad weighed the situation carefully and thought if he woke her she would move and surely would be bitten. He pulled out his pistol and took careful aim and shot the head off the rattler. The dust hit Leva in the side of the face and came out of a sleep, looked up and there was Dad with a pistol aimed right at her. She went totally into panic and ran to the house screaming. Dad ran after her but there was no stopping her.

When he got to the house Mom wouldn't even let him talk to her at first. Needless to say Leva stayed at the house the rest of the day. Dad went back to the field and brought in the snake that evening.

The kids are in order of age with oldest first. Fair, born in 1907, Alma, Easter, Leva, Ruth, Joe, Carol and Wayne, the youngest, born in 1928. At this writing all kids still survive.

In 1996 we were visiting in Bozeman and Fair admitted that if Dad hadn't worked the girls so hard they might not be here today. During our youth we all built muscles hard as rocks. Milking cows built up hand muscles so strong that when I was 21 I could crush the old tin beer cans from end to end with one hand.

Taken 1916 on Parkens Place
Left to Right – Alma, Dad, Fair, Leva, Mom and Vivian
This was supposed to be all the family John and Electa Richardson were going to have so they, planned a family portrait. Mother made all their dresses from flour sacks.

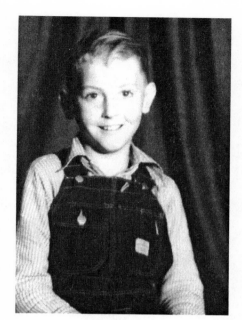

Age 7, 1935

Wayne Richardson H.S. Graduation, 1946

On leave 1946

Wayne Richardson, Age 18, H.S. Graduation

Wayne and Carol by an irrigation
canal in Mesa, by about 1995

1982 on Ascension
fishing jaunt

One of the planes I learned to fly in 1951

One of the many trains I worked on for the Milwaukee Railroad

The "Ascension"
1981 or '82

Aftermath of train wreck about
1950

Kolar yacht 58' 1982
Motored on its own bottom from
New Zealand

CHAPTER 4

TOWNSEND, MONTANA

*I*n 1939 Mr. Weaver sold the farm to Dr. Hedricks and he had other plans for the farm so we had to move again. Dad had an auction and sold everything but two days before the auction was to take place we found another farm a mile north of Townsend so we moved there. He was able to hold a few items out but for the most part everything went. This place was owned by Elmer Ward and his Mother who owned a drugstore in Helena. This place had a nice big barn with a large hayloft in it; there was a large machinery shed whereby you could back in the machinery to keep them out of most of the snow and rain. We had a nice chicken house, good double garage, a nice L shaped cattle shed behind the barn and a root cellar. The house was a two story but small. Downstairs was a living room in which we had an old leather covered couch with wooden arms. The dining area had a wood and coal stove which heated the whole house. The kitchen was small and had a pitcher pump in the corner for pumping water. Upstairs was two bedrooms with registers through the floors and the heat from the stove downstairs heated them very nicely. However we had one problem—Mother fought a bedbug infestation as long as we lived there. We treated bedding regularly to keep them down but they were in the walls and we had to seal every crack in the wood & treat them with a solvent. I think we did get rid of them eventually. Off the side of the kitchen you stepped down onto a concrete area and then into the milk room where we had another well in the corner. At first we drank the water from these wells until we found little white worms coming up in the well in the milk room. From then on we carried water for drinking from the Poor Farm which was just across the road. Knowing what we do today we could have poured a little Clorox down the well and could have killed the worms at least. Back of the milk room, but with an outside entrance, was the entrance to the bunk house. This was a log building with a sod roof and it had the most repugnant odor and we were never able to get it out. In the summer time Joe and I slept out there but even when it was cold we had to sleep with the window open because of the foul odor. Now I know in the winter we only took a bath once a week but in the summer we would go after the cows and send Shep on down to get them and we would strip off our clothes and take our bath in the Missouri using sand for soap. That old bunkhouse had been built in the 1800's, I would guess 1865 to 1890.

We had the same rental agreement as before and they were very nice people. We had two farms in this group, one right across the road from the County Poor Farm and the other ranch was one and half miles North bordering Jerry Sullivan's' farm. The lower farm had about 129 acres in it that bordered the Missouri River on the South and the upper unit was about 160 or 170 acres. We could have made some money here had my Dad managed things differently. He was a dyed in the wool dirt farmer who only knew hay, oats and wheat. My Brother Joe and Dad didn't get along very good but I will go into that later.

Living across the road from the poor farm was quite an experience in itself. Cliff and Peggy Craft ran this for the county and instead of Welfare they moved the poor and indigent out to a poor farm. They each had a room, were fed good and it was in my line of thought a better way than we have today.

Peggy was a French woman, cute with jet black hair and she started having an affair with the County Commissioner. This went on for some time when she got pregannt and Cliff finally left so she took over running the poor farm by herself and ran it for another 3 years. After that Mr. and Mrs. Duttie took over. Peggy had a daughter, Joyce, about a year older than me and I thought she was the cutest thing walking. I was so bashful and I felt so inferior to her but we always met and walked the mile to school together. I was 11 when we moved there and 16 when we left. She took tap dancing lessons and she would invite me over many times and she liked me but I was too dumb to know how to handle it. Joyce later got married had two children and died of cancer at age 31.

45

I remember one morning it was 44 below zero and I went by to walk to school with Joyce and her Mother was shocked that I didn't have a scarf over my face. She wrapped a scarf around my face and we walked the one mile to school. In Montana when we had a snow storm or it got really cold they didn't close schools. Sometimes the buses couldn't get through but most times they did.

The Poor Farm probably had 15 to 20 residents there and some of them were real characters. One old man who lived in what was known as the pest house would sit out there and just cuss up a storm by the hour. Peggy claimed that he had syphilis and his legs had dried up to where they were mummified. He sat upright in a straight backed big chair that had been reworked whereby they could slip a pale under it for his body discharges. He ate hearty and read a lot of books. For entertainment he would sit and just cuss repeatedly for a hour or more. As kids we were not allowed to go close to his house. He probably lived that way for 2 or 3 years before he deteriorated to the point that he mummified up into the hip and bowel area and he died. I remember when the country Coroner came to pick him up they wore rubber gloves and rolled him onto a rubber sheet, put him in the usual wooden coffin and they went straight to the grave yard. Peggy fumigated the house and it remained empty as long as the poor farm remained in operation.

Another old man, Ben Purdum, would take two tablespoons of Epson Salts everyday. He would walk the one mile to town everyday and the seat of his pants was always wet and brown. You didn't get down wind of him either.

Martin Surdolf was another character who chewed tobacco and always had it running down the corners of his mouth. He was quite able bodied and Dad would hire him to help during the haying and grain cutting time. I used to get so mad at him; I couldn't stand to drink out of the same water jug as he did because he would leave tobacco juice around the cap and down inside in the water. I would bring two gallon jugs of water to the field and that old bastard would find my hidden jug and drink out it. Sometimes I would get so dry that I would have to drink from it but if possible I went a half day without water. Martin kept a slop pot by his bed in his room and he would let it get full before he would empty it. He would take it out back and dump it in the Irish ditch and you could smell that all the way across the road to our house if the wind was right. Peggy Craft would get on his case regularly about that. They had indoor plumbing but he was too lazy to walk down the hall at night.

Another old man named Louie had been a logger all his life. He stood around 6' 3" or better and probably weight 230. Dad also hired Louie for Farm help and that man was powerful. He was 87 years old at that time but when he put a fork into a hay-shock, it moved. He couldn't work fast but he was one of the better old men that lived there. Remember, this was during World War II and farm help was hard to come by. We had some pretty good teams of horses and one big black percheron was a fine horse and he would work his heart out for you but don't whip him. Martin Surdolf got into it with my Dad for taking the end of the lines and laying them over the rump of Dave, the Percheron. You could just talk to that horse and he would do what you wanted but if you tapped him heavy with a line he would get so nervous that he would just shake. Dad told Louie about this characteristic and Louie got along fine with Dave.

Joe LaBree was another resident and he was one who was very clean and neat. He smoked Bull Durham tobacco and would "rolem" one after the other and always cussed them for causing him to be short of wind but he never quite. He had a 1929 Model A and for some time when Cliff and Peggy took over the Poor Farm, Joe's car was the only wheels they had.

I remember many times Joe LaBree would take his Model A and we went prospecting up Indian Creek and we came home with a few colors in the bottom of a test tube vial. It was hard work but a person could have made $10 to 20 a day panning in those days.

Joe also had a violin and Carol was taking violin lessons in school. Joe would come over in the evening and he taught Carol quite a bit about fiddling. Her music teacher heard her one day playing before class started and he was impressed with her talent.

Joe would also come over after our chores were done in the evening and we would walk down to the Missouri River and fish in the evenings. Mostly what we caught was chubs and suckers. We always had a fire going and we ate the chubs and we would bone the suckers and give them to our dog Shep. When we would pull a sucker out he knew that was his and was dancing until we got it cooked, boned and cooled for him. We had mosquitoes but by midsummer they weren't too bad.

Joe LaBree and my brother Joe became quite close friends and Old Joe wanted to go to Arizona in the worst way and he thought that might help his lung problem. He was always rolling one cigarette after another from his Bull Durham sack in his shirt pocket. Brother Joe had just turned 18 and he wanted to get away from Dad so one day they packed the old Model A and headed for Arizona. Mom cried, and so did Carol and I, but we know it had to come.

They got as far as Tremonton, Utah before the old Model A broke down. They didn't have money enough to pay for the repairs so Brother Joe got a job working on a sheep farm for Clinton Allen. Old Joe got sick and had to go to the County Hospital for treatment. I don't remember how long they stayed together but Old Joe wanted to get to Arizona in the worst way. That was the place he wanted to be when he died. Brother Joe had a job and was saving some money and he wanted to stay. Brother Joe gave Old Joe all the money he had and sent him on his way. Brother Joe remarked later that he didn't think Old Joe would live long enough to make it. I would guess he had lung cancer but I doubt if the doctors in that time even bothered to X-ray his lungs. I do know he always had a bad hacking cough.

They corresponded for a few months after Old Joe got to Arizona and then Old Joe got sick again and went to the hospital where he died. I don't know all the details but if possible I will fill them in later.

Carol and I were the last kids left at home at this time. I had just turned 13 and with Joe gone Dad took me to town and bought me a new pair of hip boots for irrigating and a new shovel. He took me to the upper ranch and taught me how to irrigate the fields and after a few days I was on my own. I had learned how to drive when I was 12 years old so by now I would take the old 29 Dodge and drive to the upper ranch at 7:00 AM and would run two heads of water till 6:00 PM. All day long I would change the water on one field and then walk to the next field and change that water. By the time you would finish with one change it was time to go back to the previous one. Bear in mind we only used canvas damns in the head ditches and we had to shovel dirt and build mud damns in the lateral ditches. Ask any full grown man who irrigated in those days and he will tell you it was back breaking work.

After a hard day in the fields we then would come home and while Dad fed the livestock, [hogs, chickens, cows & horses]; it was my job to go get the cows in and then we had to milk anywhere from four to eight cows and separate the cream from the milk. Around 8:00PM we managed to eat but some times of the year it might be closer to 9:00PM. Reveille the next morning would be 5:00 AM. This was the routine for the summer months.

How we ever managed to grow up is still a mystery. In the spring we had to clean the weeds off the ditch banks with a Martin Ditcher. This was a piece of equipment that weighed about a 1000 lbs with a heavy steel runner that sets in the bottom of the ditch and a cutting bar about 18 inches wide and eight feet long. This sets at an angle of about 45 degrees and cuts the grass and weeds from the ditch banks. Sometimes this cutter blade would strike a rock or tree root and the bar would flip to the opposite side of the ditch. My Dad would drive the team up on the bank and my job was to ride the heavy beam in the bottom of the ditch and tries to put as much weight as you could on the top end of the cutter blade. I have had this blade catch on something and flip over literally throwing me with it. If I would have been slow and been caught under it I could have gotten cut in half. Many times I and my brother Joe when he was home have been tossed like a rock and we would always land on our feet on the opposite bank. Dad would stop the team but by the time he yelled whoa and the horses stopped you would travel three to six feet.

In later years I discussed these ditchers with Don Clark who ended up being a neighbor in Mesa, AZ where we both winter after retirement. The Clark family was a neighbor of our when lived on the ranch east of Mahattan. The Clark family was responsible for get us started to going to church and later for our baptism

I did like threshing time because we had lots of activity around the farm. Dad put me on a bundle wagon which was a little easier on me because we had what was called a field pitcher who stayed out in the grain field and helped load the grain bundles on the wagons. When I got to the threshing machine I would have a few minutes to rest waiting for the wagon ahead of me to finish unloading before I got up to the thresher. During haying and threshing time neighbors would exchange work. They would come to your place and work and then when they had crops to put up you would go to their place and work. At the end you would figure up your days and you would pay them or vice versa. Women also traded labor. You might have three or four women cooking and preparing food and then when they had haying and threshing, you would go work at their ranches. It was the kid's job to stay home and do the farm chores while Dad would go trade labor. We always had the best of foods during this time and plenty of it. Several of the hired men would sleep in the barn on the hay. Dad absolutely forbids any of them to smoke in the barn.

I do think that today's youth should visit the Vista Farm Museum near Vista California or the one in Minden, Nebraska where they can get somewhat of an idea just how this country was farmed. At the museum near Vista, t hey grow grain and they have a show the last week of June and again the last week in October. They will have all antique steam engines running and will be threshing grain. It is well worth seeing even for a city-slicker.

In 1943, the land between Toston and the Three Forks junction was nothing but rank sagebrush land but they were building the Toston Dam and it was expected that they would pump water and build canals to irrigate this area. The County was selling this land for one year back taxes at 10 cents an acre. I wanted to buy 1000 acres for a $100 but my Dad would not let me do it. His reasoning was that it would just cost us $100 every year thereafter for taxes and that it was a worthless bunch of land. We didn't do it. Al McGrath, an engineer on the Milwaukee Railroad bought 2 sections of this worthless ground and he made a deal with the Fiestner boys who had a farm near the headwaters of the Missouri River. Since the Fiestner boys had all the machinery, Al made them a deal to furnish the fuel for their tractors and buy the seed wheat if they would plow under the sagebrush and plant the seed wheat. They had good conditions and the following year they harvested 40 bushels to the acre. The following year they did the same. Al then sold the land to the Kamp boys from around the Manhattan area for $50 an acre. With the profits from the crops and the land Al McGrath made $100,000. Within 10 years they had irrigation coming to part of this valley and the land values went even higher. In the 60's this land was selling for $5,000 an acre.

In 1944 in early Spring, Mrs. Ward was getting old and they decided to sell the ranches that we farmed. They offered both farms to Dad for $5500 total price. I tried to convince Dad that we could borrow the money and make it. Dad was now 61 years old and he had worked hard all his life and I think he just wanted out. He was also a poor money manager so we probably would not have made the money that we should have. If we would have grown peas, potatoes, sugar beets of something of this type I think we would have paid for those farms in a matter of 5 years.

CHAPTER 5

BOZEMAN

$\mathcal{W}$e had an auction again and everything went except a few household items. I can't be sure but I think we must have ended up with three to $5,000 total.

We moved to Bozeman and bought a house a block up the street from Leva and Glen at 506 North Montana. Now when Leva married Glen Thompson Dad had a fit. He didn't think the Thompson boys were worthy of his girls. What the hell did he expect, he wouldn't let his girls date boys and they were eighteen or better before they got to meet anyone. I understand Leva and Glen would walk down the street on opposite sides for fear someone would write back to Townsend and tell Dad. Anyway they got married and they lived in a renovated railroad boxcar down on Aspen St. Glen and Leva had fixed it up and she kept it clean as a doll house. Their two boys Dallas and Denny were born while they lived there. Glen worked construction jobs and in the winter, times got might tough. Glen was a sharp poker player and one winter he supported the family playing poker at the Stockman's Bar. Some days he would bring home $20 or better. A day's wages was maybe $5 so this was pretty good. Glen was also a good hunter so he always got his deer and elk in the Fall. Also when we would go to Bozeman to visit them Dad always threw in a ham or a side of bacon to help them out. After the kids all left home Dad was very good to help the kids.

Glen and Leva bought a little house on the corner of Montana Street and Peach Street and I think they paid somewhere in the neighborhood of $1400 for it. It took them a long time to get it paid for but they did it and Glen added porches, siding and a new roof over the years. Leva is now 93 in 2008 and still lives there.

This is where Glen and Leva lived when we moved from Townsend to Bozeman. Dad bought an old shack of a house and I was very disappointed but he was not about to spend all his savings on a house so we moved in and started renovation. All the houses in that part of town had outhouses so the first thing we did was dig an eight foot deep trench and tie into the city sewer. I was now 16 so I did a lot of the digging after school and on weekends. Dad paid about $1700 for this place which had 2 lots and then he spent another $2500 rehabbing the dump. Originally it was two old houses shoved together, so one of the first things we had to do was bring the roof up into a single gable. He hired a carpenter and we went to work. We then took one of the back bedrooms and made it into a bath room. Glen's cousin Ernie Thompson helped plumb in everything so when it was all done we could take a bath and there was room for the washing machine in there. Ernie was a good man but he made an error or two, he connected all the hot water lines to the right side of the sinks. Later Dad added on two rooms to the back of the house which gave a total of three bedrooms. For what he ended up in costs to that house we could have bought a much better home. One advantage was that when Dad got old, Leva would check on him daily as she went to work, being only one block away from us.

Montana Street was a dirt street and during the Spring thaw and heavy rains it would have ruts so deep that at times we had to park down by Leva's house so mud was something else we had to live with.

The good Lord has had his Angels watching after me a number of times. Dad was working at the Montana Flour Mill and I helped do a lot of work on the house. Dad had nailed a 2 X4 to the porch roof which had about a 2/12 pitch to it and I had a ladder above the 2 X 4 leaning against the house while I painted the gable end. I held a gallon can of paint in one hand, a brush in another and was reaching as high as I could to paint. The 2 X 4 nailer on the porch roof came loose and down came the ladder. I slid to the edge of the porch backwards, then off that and landed somewhat on my feet and then went down on my back. I was so concerned about spilling the paint that I held onto it and only spilled about a quart of it. I set the paint down and looked to my side and my arm hit a spike nail in a 2 X 4. It was then that it dawned on me that if I had landed a foot more to my left I would have landed on those spikes right in the center of my back. I thanked the Lord for that. I didn't get hurt at all but I waited for Dad to come home and then we made sure the nailers were in damned tight.

Carol got a job with Dr. Bayless in Townsend keeping house for them while we still lived in Townsend, and later went to Bozeman and ended up marrying Benny Thompson. That didn't set good with Dad to think that another daughter married another Thompson, a cousin to Glen. Benny went into the army and suffered a back injury while going through Boot Camp. He served over in the Philippines for awhile and then he was given a medical discharge.

After he got home he was in and out of the V.A. Hospital many times and suffered a lot of pain with his back. Later in the 50's he had a spinal fusion operation done by Dr. Powers in Great Falls and spent 6 weeks in a striker bed. By today's standards the fusion job was a failure and Ben suffered pain to his dying day. He did come out of it with a good pension from the VA but it wasn't worth it. He went to work for the Trident Cement Company out of Three Forks and stayed with it until he retired 30 years later. With all the criticism that Carol received for marrying Benny, he got a job and stayed with it and they retired with more income than most of the other kids. They had two children, Sharon and Dick and they each had two kids and all have done well. While in Townsend we had to get home for farm chores and when we moved to Bozeman I had lost interest. In the sixth grade I wanted to start in a band, Dad said we couldn't afford it. With this attitude and no one to encourage us kids we never got into any extra curricular school activities. I ended up taking a part time job first in a dry cleaning plant pressing men's clothes and later at Lovelace Motor Supply. This reduced the financial load on Dad because I bought all my own clothes, had my own spending money and helped with groceries. I worked from 2:30 in the afternoon to 5:00 PM after school and all day Saturday. I think my wages were around 50 cents an hour.

While working there I became a close friend of Jack Skerret, also a high school student. Behind the store Lovelace had a machine shop where they rebuilt engines and Jack's Dad was the foreman there. Jack and I would go out to Saturday night dances at May Pings and other spots around the valley.

One night we took two girls to a dance all the way over to Harrison, Montana about 70 miles away. We had Jack's Dads 1937 Ford car and as was normal, almost all Ford cars had leaky radiators. We should have filled the radiator before we left Harrison at 2:00 AM but we didn't. We had about a half case of beer left and I know we weren't supposed to be drinking but we always managed to get a little booze to go to a dance even though we were only 17 and a little wild. This night I was driving home and I noticed the engine running a little warm and not using my head very well, I would drive to the next town to see if I could get water. I could have stopped at a creek and used a beer bottle to carry water to the car. I didn't do it and by the time we reached Manhattan I thought I would use a hose from someone's lawn but their dog changed my mind. Knowing I couldn't go to the next town I then drove up the street where it was quiet and I emptied that half case of beer into the radiator. We roared on home with a cool engine. The next morning I got a call from Jack and his Dad was a little upset about how his car smelling like a stale brewery. I went to Jacks house and we drained the radiator flushed it and refilled it then washed and cleaned the car up. Jack and I spent a lot of our free time together. Every afternoon when I would get to work I would slip out to the shop and check in with him.

One day not too long after that Jack told me at school that John Lovelace had told him that he was going to send Jack to a school where he would learn machinist work. He was very much elated over this. Two days later I went to work at 2:30 and just as I walked into the shop door there was an explosion and Jack was laying against a wall with a gash about 2 inches wide that reached from his eyebrows to the back of his head. The brain was still pulsing but for all practical purposes he was dead. The ambulance came and removed him and then John Lovelace made me go out there and hose down all the blood and clean up the place. At that young age I was devastated.

What happened was a carbide generator had blown up. In those days we used this piece of equipment to generate acetylene which is used for welding. To charge these units, you fill a large tank with water, then you fill a smaller container on the top with carbide. There is a gauge on it and you regulate the pressure in the tank by the amount of carbide that is released into the water. In this case Jack goofed and when he closed the top cover all the carbide dropped into the water at once. Within minutes or maybe seconds the pressure built up to explosive pressure. It blew so hard that the carbide holder on top went through the roof and into the air maybe 300 feet and then came down through the roof of Dyes Plumbing shop 100 feet away. A man there was walking across the shop room and when this piece came through the roof it hit his shoe heel and tore it off, but no injuries.

I took my Dads' old 1929 dodge car to High School in October to overhaul the engine as my first project for shop. We only had one hour a day to work on it and by the time you got your tools out and then cleaned up you worked 30 minutes. It took me until early spring before I finished it. After we got the engine done we then decided to paint it and that took another month. In those days a good paint job was considered to be done in lacquer paint and then rubbed down. Rubbing it down is a bitch of a job. It never did look like a pros job.

Dad Kind of let me take over the car so I drove it to school and also got to chase around at night with it. I also ran around with George Gillette, whose Dad was the Fire Chief; and one night we were driving around town in a snow storm with flakes as big as quarters, when we noticed an ambulance heading out towards the four corners. We could hardly see to tell where the middle of the road was but being kids we followed. About 3 miles out town a head-on collision had occurred. Four kids in one car and 3 in the other one had collided head-on in this blinding snow storm, all of the kids from our High School. One young man who had lost his parents and had inherited quite a bit of money, drove a new 1941 Chevrolet car and was a little on the wild side but a nice guy. The other car was a 1939 Lincoln and owned by an executive of the local bank. His daughter Jacqueline was in the Lincoln and her head was caught have half way through the windshield and had cut her ear to ear around the chin.

Another girl, Evelyn Harrison was thrown through the windshield of Marvin's Chevrolet and was lying in a ditch with water in it and gurgling in the water before she could be pulled out. Her nose was laid out on each side of her face. All the other kids suffered broken arms or legs and all survived. Marvin was the only fatality. By the time we got there we weren't able to help too much because the ambulance crew had things pretty well under control. They couldn't get them all in the ambulance so we hauled two who were not hurt much into the hospital. They think the snow was so bad that the kids were driving with only parking lights on thinking they could see better.

On the lighter side of things, the Police Station was the on the corner of Main and Rouse Streets and in a town of only 12000 people and most of them law abiding citizens, four of us boys took two blocks of wood and lifted up the rear of the police car sitting in front of the station and set the blocks under the rear axels. We then went to a pay phone across the street at the Bozeman Hotel and reported a fight at the Stockman's Bar. We laughed for weeks about the cops coming out and racing the engine and the car didn't go anywhere.

During this era, we went to dances at May Pings which was a popular Saturday night stomping place. Everybody would have a few drinks and dance to a little three piece band.

Usually it was Ernie Thompson as the drummer and a guitar and a piano as the music or other piece for the band. Ernie, in my opinion, was one of the best little drummers in the area. He didn't try to drown out the rest of the band, he would use wire brushes a lot. The band was loud enough to hear but it didn't cause hearing loss in your older years. The bands in Montana in those days played western and old time music. At the Eagles they would play a two step, a waltz or two, a schottische, and a square dance that didn't have 68 different calls. They were very enjoyable evenings. I looked a little older than my age and May Ping would sell me booze so long as I didn't get drunk and cause any problems.

Rarely did you see violence at May Pings and if you did, it was fists and the winner usually helped the loser back inside and would buy him a drink. In my case I didn't get a drink. May had two out-houses out back and the ladies would have to use the outhouse, but being dark most of the men would go back of their outhouse and pee on the ground. I had stepped outside the back door and there was a guy beating the hell out of a woman not more than 110 pounds. She was bleeding at the nose and cuts on her face and I was afraid he would kill her. I jerked his shoulder back and brought one from low down and layed him out on the ground. I then jumped on him giving him some more and berating him for hitting a woman. She pulled off her high heeled shoe and started beating me over the head with it and informed me in no uncertain terms that I was hurting her husband. I managed to get up and yelled at him to get up and kill that bitch, she needs it.

I learned a lesson right there; never stick your nose into someone else's problems.

Since then I have also formed that opinion all the way to Governments. We shouldn't be running around trying to tell the rest of the world how to live. I'll touch on this again when I get to Turkey

CHAPTER 6

NAVY TIME

*W*hen I was 18 we knew the war was over but four of us High School boys thought we would like to get in on what we could of seeing the world. We had more than enough credits to graduate so we all enlisted in the Military. Sam Cloninger and I went into the Navy and ended up together at the San Diego Naval Training center. After boot camp we kept in touch by letters. Sam ended up in Georgia as a Corpsman in a hospital and I went to an engineering school at Great Lakes, Illinois. After that I was shipped to Boston and served aboard the John W. Haynsworth, DD-700.

I rather enjoyed my time in Boston and at times I spent a dime and would keep getting transfers and I rode the entire network. I would get off check out that part of town, get back on and go some more. Subways were kind of a new thing for a Montana boy who had never ridden on one. During this time I met a nice girl named June and we enjoyed each other's company. I might have married that girl except she was diabetic, so I got cold feet.

During this time our skipper told us that the ship had to be painted but we only had a short to do it or we have to do it in New Orleans where it would be much hotter. The Navy yard in Boston had tons of paint stacked about half way between our dock and the main gate, our exit when we would go on liberty. He suggested that we might liberate some of that paint as we returned from liberty. Everybody cooperated so we loaded the ship holes up with five gallon cans of paint. It being dark when we returned from liberty, we would just grab one or two five gallon pales of paint and bring it to our ship and we ended up with plenty of gray paint but also reds, orange, yellow etc. The ship got painted inside and out and when we left we just carried the extra paint up on our pier the morning we left and cast off.

We left Boston three months later and headed for New Orleans. War time compliment on this ship was 300 men, peace time was 160. We left with only 90 men on board which required us to work 12 on and 12 off shifts. Our Captain asked us and it was a voluntary thing to get us all to New Orleans, which we were all anxious to do. Right out of Boston and until we got to Cape Hatteras we encountered a vicious storm and two Italian boys, Groppi and Serri got so sea sick that they laid between the water tanks and the boiler and could hardly lift their heads to barf in a bucket. They lost about twenty pounds body weight on that trip. Oliver, a Water Tender 3rd handled both checks for boiler water level control, Stony, a 30 year Chief and I, a Fireman 2nd, handled the burners. For three days we were listing 35 to 45 degrees every roll. Oliver could sit down on a bucket and he tied himself to a stanchion and under a steady speed he didn't have too much to do. Stony and I changed off on burner watch and we had rags tied to a stanchion and then around our waist, with the left hand we hung on to the Micrometer burner control valve. Stony would sit on a rag can and I would tie him with rags to a stanchion and he would get a little sleep. Then when I got to where the gauges were blurring, he would stand watch and I would sleep. Every wave the bow would dip under and the ship would shudder and then when it crested, the screws would kick out and you would think it was going to disintegrate, thus the name Tin Can must have originated.

Every minute the bridge sounded the horn as is required in inclement weather. Then the last night out our horn sound was a rather high pitch, then immediately a low pitched fog, horn type sound answered, and then a bell from the bridge gave us a flank reverse. Talk about something to get your adrenaline moving, I was throwing extra burners in those boilers as fast as I could move. The next morning we found out that we had missed broad-siding a freighter by less than 20 feet.

The previous day our sister ship the Waldron, DD-699, caught a wave wrong and it split a seam on the starboard side flooding the forward engine room. The repair crews were down there welding deck plates or anything they could get across the break. They thought they were going to lose the ship but they saved it. A day later we steamed into Charleston,

South Carolina and the Waldron was on a 10 degree list. We had to stay there for three months while they made repairs.

While we were there, our Chief, Stony who was in charge of the fire-room told me, "kid if I had not have had you to help we would have been in deep trouble getting this ship in here." The sea was so rough that none of us felt great but I always had a good appetite. They had the same problem in the aft fire room and a kid of German decent named Heineman was also one who got sick. After arriving in Charleston my Old Stony said kid I want you to take the test for Fireman 1st class. I studied a few days and a bunch of us took the test. I passed and Heineman failed. This made him angry and every time he would see me he would start swinging on me.

I wasn't much of a fighter and he had 20 pounds or better on me to my 155, and I was 6' 1" to his 5' 10", so he had my face swollen from one side to the other from four fights. One night he came in from liberty at midnight half drunk just as I was coming off watch and he caught me in the washroom (head) and told me he was going to kill me. I had a little one celled flashlight in my hand which had a safety pin on it and he lit into me. I guess I thought he was going to kill me so I really got with it, fighting for everything I had. The safety pin came open and punctured through my ring finger on my right hand and each time I hit him it was leaving a hole in his face. I had him unconscious and was dragging him out to the fantail and was trying to roll him into the Mississippi river when someone caught me and stopped me. They hauled him up to Sick Bay where he stayed for several days recuperating from broken jaw bones, cracked ribs, and one hole almost cost him an eye. After he got out of Sick Bay he apologized and tried to be my friend but I wanted nothing to do with that son-of-a-bitch. He never bothered me again. This never got to the Captain because but everyone knew how he had worked me over.

We finally arrived in New Orleans in May of '47. We spent the next six months taking reserve sailors out for two week cruises to Cuba, Jamaica and one trip to Nassau.

Most of these were enjoyable but one time as we were coming back to New Orleans we followed a hurricane up the Mississippi. Large boats were washed up on land, houses of the river dwellers were destroyed and when we got to New Orleans the town was a mess. We had to hook up our ships to the city power systems to furnish power for about half the town.

My enlistment ended while I was in New Orleans and they shipped me to Pensacola, Florida for discharge. I should have re-upped but I didn't and I went home to make my way on the open employment market. Sam Cloninger went back to school and graduated as a radiologist doctor.

Later I was in Chicago on a trip and called my old friend Sam Cloninger but he was so tied up with work that I only got to visit on the phone. Thirty some years later I went into the Bozeman graveyard to visit my Dad's grave and there by the entrance gate was a large stone reading Samuel Cloninger. I found that he had developed severe arthritis conditions and at 40 he had to walk with a cane and at the age of 49 he died.

After I got out of the Navy I came home and joined the 52/20 club as military men knew it that got home. This meant that we could draw $20.00 a week for 52 weeks after discharge. For awhile Freddie Christopherson, Al Williamson and I enjoyed the good life. Living at home and beer being 25 cents each we did enjoy a couple of months of this. During this time I signed up for the GI Bill on education and learned how to fly at the Bozeman airport. Bozeman Aviation with Dick Hill, Tom Price and Mac McCall were our instructors. All a group of men who had been B-17 Pilots and saw lots of action in WWII. We used to stop at the Belgrade Lounge to have a beer after flying and the day that I soloed, Al Williamson, Betty Hill, [Dick's Sister} and I went in for a beer on me of course. It was the custom in these days to roll the dice for drinks using horses as the game, double or nothing for drinks. I had to roll for three drinks at a time and I won 23 rolls before I lost. Jack the owner, said Wayne you are going to stay all night or until you lose a round. I lost the 24th. Luckily traffic was not like it is today because we drank up got into our car and drove to Bozeman. I always did have the ability to drive straight when drinking and I never had an accident. Once while I was still in High School four of us kids went to Walt Brainard's wedding reception at the Dry Creek School House, I drank straight whiskey and drove all the way back to Bozeman in low gear in a '29 Dodge so I wouldn't drive too fast. That is the only two times that I can recall when I drove drunk. Many times we had drinks at a dance and drove home but not drunk like these two times.

CHAPTER 7

RAILROADING

*T*he 52/20 club didn't last long for me, My brother-in-law Fred Coombs suggested I go to Deer Lodge and apply for a job as a fireman on the Milwaukee Railroad. I did and they hired me. Then Fred suggested I go to Lewistown, Montana and work on the branch line where they used all steam engines. I did and for two years I fired steam engines and on some runs Ernie Ford didn't have anything on me, I have shoveled 16 tons of #9 coal many days and on some days when the run could last up to 16 hours, I have emptied two, fifteen ton tanks of coal a day. After two years I had enough seniority to work part time on the main line where it was all an electrified system with very little work for the fireman to do. It did benefit me to know steam because when work got scarce on the main line I would hook up my trailer and go back to the branch line and work. Today I see old steam engines with nostalgia but 50 years ago I felt like the Lord or Devil would be waiting for me and have me shoveling coal again.

While I worked on the railroad we had some good times. In Lewistown it was rather quiet and I did some roller-skating with a girl named Betty Berg. She was a little bit on the plump side but a great skating partner. On Halloween one year we won first prize for doing the circle waltz on skates.

A few years later in 1949, when I was just 21, I was working in engine service in Lewistown, I didn't have the best rapport with the local Police. I think I only got one ticket in 2 years but we had a bastard named Brutus who was a Motorcycle cop and you had to watch him. I had this 1940 Ford custom coupe with two chrome air horns mounted on the front fenders, the body under-slung two inches, smitty mufflers and chrome tail pipes coming out just above the rear bumper. One time I was cruising down Main Street in my shiny little car about 15 miles per hour with a cute little brunette named Betty snesseled by my side and my arm around her, This Brutus pulled up alongside of me and said, "Heh Mack use two hands", to this I replied, "I can't I have to use one to drive with." He hauled me into the Police station and it cost me $15.00.

On another occasion, I was driving down Main Street on Ice when a County Snowplow ran through a stop sign and the blade sliced my cute little coupe from the front bumper to the rear. The County refused to pay for repairs and my insurance company paid for it.

We would always park our cars in the Round-house when we were out on a run and on another occasion someone had pushed my car forward just enough that when the Hostler ran an engine in the Roundhouse it hit the front of my car. Again my insurance company, State Farm, repaired my car and canceled my insurance. Some railroader didn't like me and they had shoved my car forward, I am sure, just enough so the engine hit it when parking it in the Roundhouse. Even when I was running an engine, Hostling, I knew where my clearances were and I never ran an engine into anything or through the Round House wall, but I have seen where it happened. A hostler on the railroad is an advanced fireman who knows how to run a locomotive but has not met all the requirements for road service, so they run engines around the yard, got them ready for the road crews and put them in the Roundhouse when they came in off a run.

It seems that from the time I was a little kid up until I was 40 years old or better, I had a way of doing things or saying things that caused people to get upset with me. I used to pray to God to help me create a more likeable personality. I always felt that I was inferior or just plain dumb. When you have an inferiority complex it is tough. Maybe it was because we grew up so poor and were called names in school, I don't know. Anyway when I reached middle age I began to develop a more extrovert personality and it paid off. God sure took a long time to help me. I have prayed so many times for things and they always came to pass but usually it `took a few years to get them answered. I remember when I was young, of wanting to travel and see the world but I knew in my heart that I would never be able to afford it; then out of the blue sky I was offered a job in Turkey and for the next eight years I traveled through 25 countries.

This will be covered later after I left the Montana Power Company.

Bud Richards and I needed to save money during the winter when we were layed off so we rented an apartment together at a motel. We must have batched together for over a year. One or the other of us was out on the road a good share of the time. Today if you did that eyebrows would raise but there everyone knew we weren't queer. Talk about an odd couple, I was Felix and he was Oscar. He would come in off a run and take a bath in the tub and it would be black with coal dust and he never cleaned it unless I got on his ass. Dirty dishes would be piled in the sink and mud on the floor. I would clean up the house and leave it that way when he came in. He was a terrible slob. One time I came in off a run in the heat of summer and there on the counter was butter, milk, ham and much more. I opened the refrigerator door and from the top shelf to the bottom was Budweiser beer. I was so furious that I just sat down and tried to drink space back in the refrigerator. I wasn't the drinking man that Bud was so after about three beers I moved the beer out to make room for groceries. Fortunately they were not spoiled.

Bud's Dad was a foreman at the Hanover plaster plant and one winter when I was laid off on the railroad I went out to work there and the only job they would give me was a sackers job in the mill. I was working with George, a small man with some Indian blood line in his ancestry. He was the toughest man I ever knew. We would sack 94 lb sacks, load them on a hand truck eight high, which was just up to my nose and I am 6'1, and then truck them out to a box car. We would load a row to eight high in the car and then we would gang together and throw them twelve high in the box car. Many days we loaded three car loads out at 800 sacks to the car. I worked there for more than four months and for the first three weeks I would go home, bath, fix dinner and go to bed. After that I had built some ripples in my stomach muscles and could go to a Saturday night dance or something. I thought shoveling 15 tons of coal into a fire box was tough, I soon found out what tough meant. I don't remember George's last name but he did say later that I was the only man they ever sent out with him that could handle the job. Size isn't everything either, George was as tough a guy as I have ever known and one day when three sacks in a row exploded while they were being filled, he grabbed it off the spout and threw it a good 25 feet down the hall. It still weighed around 90 lbs because they never exploded until they were almost full. When filling these sacks you had to keep working the top of the sack to expel air or pressure would build up and blooey, they would explode.

While I worked there Bud Richards' dad and I went fishing one evening after work. Bud looked up the creek and recognized the game warden coming toward us. Bud said, stay right here and keep fishing till I'm gone. He took off running up the hill towards the house with the warden in chase. Bud ran till he was winded and he stopped. The Warden said OK I gotcha, where is your license? Bud pulled out his license and showed him and it was then that the Warden realized that it was me who he wanted. I was long gone.

I paid Mrs. Richards $1 a day for my lunch and believe me I got my moneys' worth. She put out good food and plenty of it so I hung on a heavy nosebag. I might explain to any city slickers who might by chance be reading this, when we were working our horses in the fields we had made a feeder out of a gunny sack by fastening a rope on each side of the sack. We would fill it with their ration of oats and hang it over their head behind the ears. It being porous they could breathe OK and they didn't spill their oats on the ground. It's called a nose bag. Their hay could be on the ground and it wouldn't get destroyed. Our horses were working hard so they had to be fed well.

While I lived in Lewistown, Montana I had a little 65 HP Taylor craft plane. Bud and I both had a private license so on Sundays we would pick up a dozen newspapers and air drop them to friends that we knew in the country around there. We got pretty good at it because in a good share of the cases we would come in low and drop them right near the door, but most of the time in the yards. No, we never hit a window, luckily. That was one way to keep current on our required flying time. Fortunately we never got into trouble for flying under 500 feet over a house while delivering papers.

Spring Creek ran right through Lewistown and it was renowned as being an excellent trout stream with some large ones in it. I wish I could go back to that time now because I would do more fishing.:

After WWII, I worked for the Milwaukee Railroad on the branch line out of Lewistown as a fireman on the steam locomotives for two years.

On one particular trip we were returning on a run from Great Falls to Lewistown. At that time they had a two car passenger train that also ran from Lewistown to Great Falls and back.

On this particular trip Jerry Gillen was my engineer and we had coaled and watered up at

Square Butte and headed up the hill toward Coffee Creek with enough time to get to Coffee Creek and into the siding ahead of the passenger train. When we got to the top of the hill we knew the passenger train had to stop at Coffee Creek to pick up mail, baggage and passengers.

Jerry said to me, "On these tracks they can't run any faster than we can, let's go to Denton ahead of them, "So, he let-er roll. Now there were eight or ten passengers on the platform, we had just topped the Square Butte hill and was now freewheeling down grade with a rope of black smoke coming from our stack. The passenger platform was not more than 3 ft. or so from the tracks. As we went by the one thing that caught my eye on the fireman's side was a pretty girl in a nice white (Marilyn Monroe style dress) (Girls wore nice dresses in those days), and the dust and smoke just covered the station. Her dress was going up around her waist and she was squatting to hold it down. No doubt about it the dust and smoke was terrible.

We made it to Denton and were in the siding in plenty of time so the passenger train had no delays, but when we arrived at the Roundhouse in Lewistown, they were waiting for us.

Jerry got his Butt chewed good with threats of losing his job if he ever pulled a stunt like that again. We went down to the local watering hole on our way home and had a couple of beers to sooth our nerves.

We also used to go to Hilger out of Lewistown for their Saturday night dances and also to Grass Range.

When the summer work opened up at Three Forks I went back to the Main Line on the Milwaukee. I was going to lay around for awhile and rest up. I was sitting in Fred's bar one afternoon nursing a cold beer when Steve McDonald came in looking for farm labor. No one was available that would work and he said Wayne come out and help me get the hay up, It's on the ground and we have to get it stacked. I said no I just came down from Lewistown where I had been working hard enough shoveling coal into steam engines. He said, these lazy bastards around here won't work. I said now wait a minute about who is a lazy bastard. He said, when will you be going back on the railroad, I said about a week, so he said come on out for that week. I went to my room gathered some clothes and we headed up the Madison Valley to their ranch. I helped put up the hay, then the grain was ready to combine so I helped with that. I stayed for a month and I am very happy that I did. The railroad got busy and they insisted that I come back to work.

After I left the branch line in Lewistown and returned to the main line running out of Three Forks. We had a few exciting moments. On one particular trip my engineer was Tommy Whalen, the head brakeman was Jimmy Carlson, Conductor was Chuck Adams and I don't remember the rear brakeman's name.

Tommy Whalen was a nice old guy but he should never have been allowed to be an engineer. He had absolutely no mechanical aptitude and to be in a position pulling a train you need to have a feeling of how your train is handling, know what the limits are on you air braking system, and a multitude of other things.

On this particular trip we were returning from Deer Lodge to Three forks with about a 3500 ton train pulled with a four unit electric locomotive. This part of the Milwaukee system was an all electrified division. We had to cross the continental divide out of Butte, Montana which was about 12 miles up the west side and 22 miles down the east side, all at 2% grade. Going up the mountain we traveled about 16 to 18 MPH and when you tipped over the top the engineer would switch controls into regeneration, whereby you pumped electricity back into the power lines and this would serve as your braking system holding your train at about 18 MPH going down the east side. On this day we had an electrical fault somewhere in the traction motors of the locomotive and it kicked out leaving you in freewheeling. Normally a good engineer immediately starts drawing off air to slow the train down and a good engineer can hold the braking system on what is known as "the hump" and control his system to come down on air brakes, stopping once or twice to cool the brakes.

I kept a pretty close eye on Tommy's controls but then I went back through the engine to check the back units and I noticed the air pressure was down to 60 pounds which to me was 10 pounds less than it should have been. Jimmy and I both noted the conductor and brakeman going over the top at the rear of the train tying down hand brakes. I ran to the front and told Tommy we are gaining speed, use your engine driver brakes. I went back to start tying down hand brakes. Jimmy was already on top of the first car. I ran at a crawling running position to the next car and would tie down the hand brake, then on to the next one. Jim and I both considered jumping but the speed now was fast enough that we thought it was death either way. The cars were rocking so much we had a hard time just going to the next car to tie down brakes.

We ended up getting six cars tied down on the front of the train, all loaded cars and the conductor and rear brakeman got 12 cars tied down on the rear. We finally noticed the train start to slow down. We thanked God and headed back to the engine.

When we got back to the cab I pulled the speed recorder open and it showed that we had reached a maximum speed of 45 MPH and had traveled about 14 miles before the train came to a stop. The maximum speed a freight train was supposed to come off that mountain was 22 MPH.

The conductor was on his way forward from the caboose and he was mad. He cussed the engineer out with everything that he had been taught not to say when growing up.

I had gloves on so my hands came off without damage, but my jacket was torn, my elbows badly skinned, my overall knees were torn open and both knees badly skinned but we all survived so we felt lucky.

Tommy pumped up the train air brakes again and the conductor rode the front end the rest of the way into Three Forks. We released the hand brakes and creeped the rest of the way about 6 or 8 miles to get to get off the mountain.

In 1955 the Milwaukee Railroad was about to go under. The last year I worked there I think I only put in three months work. In part of 53 and 1954 I filled in operating high voltage substations which furnished power for the electrified division over the Rockies. By today's standards on safety in the 90's, they would close them down immediately. We were put to work with only a few shifts with a seasoned operator and then a shift was turned over to us working all alone. At East Portal a young kid who wanted to have his units looking spic and span, had climbed up on one of the 100KV transformers to clean the dust off the insulating bells. He dusted them about half way up and there to this day was his hand print on the insulating bell where the voltage jumped to him and fried him. I had some experience working on electric locomotives as a fireman so I knew safety. When you would be putting out maximum amperes to the DC trolley for a train coming up a mountain, a traction motor on an engine might flash over and this would flash over our commutator's on the substations generators creating an explosion like a rifle going off at your back. You had to stand right in front of them in order to watch the meters on the board and be ready to make a change.

Another safety hazard was behind the main board where you had to go to read a couple of meters and you had to pass right by a 4400 volt transformer that furnished power for the railroad signal system. This transformer sat on the floor and was about five feet tall with no guard rails or screens around it. When we walked back there we made darn sure to keep our hands and arms down.

Another dandy was when you had to perform maintenance on the breakers which sat on a frame work on top of the switch board. We could de-energize the breakers but we could not de-energize the bus bars that ran through a frame work at our feet. We had two 2 X12 planks lying on the frame work which cleared the 3400 DC bus network below by about 6 inches. If you should slip while working on the breakers above and slip off the 2 X 12's, sayonara, you had six inches clearance before you hit a ¾ X 6 inch wide copper bus. Again we were very careful. I went up to the East Portal sub in November with Jean, my wife. The snow was four feet deep and when we came out in May the snow was fourteen feet deep. Every day we had about 30 minutes of snow shoveling to keep our walk-way clear. Once a week, we had to climb up on the roof and shovel the snow off the house roof.

We had four families up there, the section or track maintenance couple and three couples who operated the Power House. Once a week we would all gather at one house, except the man on shift, and have a dinner, all of us dressed in nice clothes. After dinner we would play penny-anti poker or something and it was enjoyable.

Sometimes cabin fever would set in and we would trade shifts with another to get a day off. To make up for this we would have to work 16 hours straight to make up for the day off. Now you're asking yourself, where would someone go on their day off up there. I only did this once that winter, so Jean and I put on our snow shoes and headed down to the highway 4 miles away. The Greyhound bus schedule that we had was out of date and they had changed their times. We waited at the little Taft Hotel at the bottom of the hill and no bus. The old couple that ran it was gone and after about two hours a man came along with an old surplus 4 X 4. He made his money pulling trucks and cars with trailers over the mountain when they would spin out. He had a string across his windshield and it was full of wedding bands, diamonds and watches and every sentence he began started with, "I were". It was getting late in the day so he quit and gave us a ride all the way to Wallace, Idaho and he would not take any money. We checked into a hotel and stacked our snowshoes along with a bunch of skis. We went to a local bar and had a couple of drinks but didn't know anyone and the couple of old drunks in there didn't excite our appetite for conversation.

We then went to a movie and went back to the hotel and bed. The next day we walked around town, learned a bit of the history about the mining in Wallace and the Cat House. We caught the only bus at 7:00 Pm and headed home. When we showed the bus driver where to let us off, he was appalled and said that if the passengers didn't mind he was going to wait till we got upon that nine foot snow bank. Some of the passengers remarked as we went up the aisle, how can you make that little woman get off here in the night. My God there is nothing around here. I assured them that we were safe and that we only had ten animals up there that we knew of. I finally had to stop and give them a little speech. I told them that we had a nice warm home up on top of that mountain where we worked operating a high voltage substation which furnished power for the electric trains, and yes the snow is 14 feet deep up there, yes we do have five coyotes, three bobcats and two Mountain Lions and that is all that we know of. If a Lion should show aggressiveness I would pull out this flare or fussee as is known on the railroad and strike it. No animal will attack fire. We got out, unloaded our snowshoes and a little piece of rope. I shoved three of the snowshoe handles into the bank and started Jean up, she shoved the last one in as she got up to the top and away she went. I tied the rope onto the others and started up and would pull the rope to disengage the bottom one etc. It took less than five minutes. Some of the people got off the bus and they all gave us a roaring send off when we got to the top. We used to snowshoe down that mountain to the highway, four miles in 50 minutes but going up it always took one hour and 30 minutes.

On a few other occasions we would just snowshoe down to the Taft hotel, visit with the old couple, play the juke box and have a couple of drinks, a bit to eat and go home. The worst part of the whole winter were the electrical explosions when the commutators would flash-over caused by a locomotive. Another thing that could cause these flashovers was when they were pulling a tonnage train and the engineer might let the engine driver wheels slip a little. A little snow on a rail can cause this slippage. Most good engineers with these kinds of conditions would keep his hand at ready on the sanding valve.

Trains would not stop for us on top of the mountain unless you had a medical emergency. So to get our groceries we would radio down to

Missoula to a certain store where he kept his ham radio on at all times. Give him your list of groceries and he would pack them in a box and take them to the train depot where they were loaded on the baggage car of the passenger train. The baggage man had a rope tied to the wall at one side of the sliding baggage door, then he had a pulley attached to the other side of the door frame. He would stack our groceries near the door with this rope on the back side of the boxes and threaded through the pulley on the other side of the door. At our station we had shoveled out a shelf in the snow about four feet high on the right side of the tracks and had a flag stuck in the snow bank twelve feet before our shelf. When the baggage man saw that flag he would pull like hell and the groceries would slide out the door and onto our snow shelf. All that winter, I think we had two eggs broken and that was it.

One night while I was on shift at about 1:00 AM, all was shut down because no trains were in the area. I heard an awful scream like a woman. I ran outside there it was again, I went up by each house, walked up to their doors and all I could here was a snore in a couple of houses. I then decided that I would go to my house and make a sandwich and then I went back to the substation.

The next morning I thought I should shovel the snow off my roof so I got my snow shoes and shovel out and up I go. When I got up there I noticed these big cat tracks right above my porch and a butt mark where he had sat down. I wondered if he had been there when I walked up to my house. At least he wasn't hungry I presume.

Next spring when we got back to Three Forks people often would ask what you do for entertainment. I used to tell them that we make our own. We had some of the best fishing holes in the area, we would go out in the country and shoot gophers and sometimes we would go help a rancher haying or branding for a weekend. One weekend I was in Willow Creek helping Jack Fitzhugh get some horses in. We got them into a corral and then they tried roping them. One little filly was just shaking as she would circle around on my side. I said hold it guys and I grabbed a lead rope and stepped off the poles into the corral and I talked to her and she came right up to me and I put the rope around her neck and led her out. She was just shaking and wanted to know that no one was going to hurt her. Jack and the boys were totally flabbergasted.

For entertainment one evening, we got restless looking for mischief. Our town had a whorehouse in the Western hotel and so we thought it would be funny to light off a cherry bomb fire cracker in the lobby. It was about 9:00 PM so we went to the restaurant, got a #10 tin can so we wouldn't damage the floor in the hotel. We drew straws to see who would run in and drop the fire cracker and Jack Barger lost. Jack took the cherry bomb and the can, lit a cigarette and headed inside while Tommy Tomkens, Jimmy Carlson and I waited in the car. He ran in and fortunately no one was in the lobby, he sat the can down, lit the bomb, dropped it in the can and ran like hell to the car. Just as he got back to the car the bomb exploded and we roared off down to the gravel pit about a ½ mile straight down the street. When we got down there we caught our local wife of one of the saloon owners and they were making mad passionate love. She made us promise not to tell her husband, so we all agreed and left. Everybody in town knew that was going on anyway. We drove around to the East end of town and came in on the highway from Whitehall. We drove by and stopped to see what all the commotion was out in front of the Western Hotel and all the people from the Bryant Hotel were also out there. The night Marshall was Phil Fulcher, a fireman who was laid off and had taken that job to fill in. He came over to the four of us and asked if we knew anything about what had happened. We answered no, that we had just come back from Whitehall, but we came back with what happened? Phil said the madam had called in claiming that someone had shot at her with a shotgun, but he said he thought it was just a prank because he could smell fire cracker smoke.

Three Forks had a population of 1100 people and had seven bars so you can see what the local pastime was at times. Our local priest would call up the wives of many railroaders sometimes before the train would be out of town and would have them come down for prayer at the rectory, or sometimes he would go to their house. One night he went to a house and when he went to leave at 1:00 AM his car wouldn't start. I know all these things because to get a number you had to pick up the receiver and the operator would ask, "number please," and I was a good friend of the operator.

One night we came back into town and thought we would stop at the Sacajawea bar for a nightcap. It was locked tight at 9:30 PM but the lights were on. We were able to peek in and there was our local priest drinking and having a ball with five of our local wives.

Another night a bunch of the boys were whooping it up and there was one of our local girls there. Through all the drinking they started betting about who had the longest dong. Well a man stood at the end of the bar and stretched it out and a notch was carved in the bar with his initials. If a guy didn't rise to the occasion he got to rub it up against H?? (with no Panties) to get a rise. The Barber I believe won first prize.

While I lived in Three Forks, I have to say I had never matured. Looking back today I wonder how I could have been so dumb. I ran with the railroaders there and the single ones all drank a little. A couple of the high school girls were quite friendly with me but I was 22 and these kids were 17, so I viewed them as kids. However, Paul and Betty moved there from Van Nuys, California and bought the Texaco station on the corner. Paul had wanted to get out of the rat race which was his motive for moving up to Montana. They had a daughter named Patty and she was the cutest little blond gal in town. One day I had just come in off a run and Paul asked me if I wanted to go through Yellowstone Park with them. We had a nice trip for the day and Patty and I had nice conversations, but dumb me, I guess I looked upon her as a queen, untouchable by me. Later Paul offered to take part of the building next to the station and set me up in a linoleum floor covering business, no rent until I got it on a paying basis. It could have expanded to all kitchen equipment, but I had never been in business before and was afraid of failure, so I declined. Now I just told you I was dumb about certain things and what I couldn't see was that he was looking for a husband for Patty. Looking back, I should have grabbed that deal. Not long after that Paul had been having lunch at Veeda's Café and when he left, he got to the front door and remarked that he was sure short of breath.

He dropped dead from a heart attack.

CHAPTER 8

MONTANA POWER CO.

*A*fter that I married a young widow in Three Forks, named Jean and she was the best companion a man could have and the best lover this side of heaven. If I went fishing or hunting she was not to be left behind. If we went to a formal ball she was dressed with the finest and a beautiful dancer. One problem, after four years of marriage, I had slowed down to about three or four times a week rather than the daily or multi-daily episodes. Then while we were in Great Falls and I was working for the Montana Power Company I found that she couldn't keep her pants up. Another divorce. Another wife that six months later came around and begged me to come back. I had to sell the new house furnished and I gave Jean our little Karman Ghia as her share of the settlement. I had bought her an electric organ because she wanted to learn to play one and I was able to sell that for what I owed on it. I was the only one that learned to play anything on it.

I had been laid off from the railroad when I went to Great Falls and hired out with the Power Company as a laborer on a real widow-maker of a job for $1.97 per hour. The Rainbow Dam was an old wooden dam built around 1916 over rocks and some concrete. The wooden 12 X 12 beams were spiked to cross members over an underlay of large rocks. In time the rocks had somehow deteriorated or sunk into the river bed to the point that large holes existed under the beams. The 18 to 24 inch spikes had worked themselves up until four to six inches of spike were sticking up above the beams and the beams were covered with wet moss.

If a person should slip and lose his safety line those spikes would have ripped you a new butt. We used safety lines tied to the upright top of the dam and had to work our way down the moss covered beams, chain-saw holes through the beams and pour concrete into the rock area underneath. I remember one hole where we poured nearly 100 yards of concrete. It is a wonder that during the high water season that the dam didn't give way. After we poured the concrete we would drive the spikes down with a 10 pound sledge.

To get off the dam we had to walk to one end across a spillway which was always leaking enough water to make it mossy slick. We always tried to walk as close to the gate wall as possible but this one evening I slipped and down the spillway I went flying. At the bottom the concrete spillway curved up which gave me a lift into the air about 20 feet and ker-splash I landed in a large pool of water. The rest of the crew were really worried but I swam to the bank and walked out unhurt.

After about a month on this job I was stopped one evening on the road, by Cliff Daniels, who had checked my background and asked me to report to work the next morning at Black Eagle Dam. I started as an assistant operator on the turbine floor and within 90 days I was used as a relief control room operator. I was encouraged to enroll in night school at the local college and I have not been sorry for that to this day. It took me five years at night time to finish but I ended up with a BS ASC in Electrical.

After five years the profit structure of the Power Company was not too good so they started to weed out the deadwood, some employees had been with the company 18 years. I was not going to be laid off but I was being demoted from a distribution dispatcher, past a control room operator, and an assistant operator but all the way back to a laborer pulling trash off the dam.

I had worked afternoon shift the night before and slept in a little. At about 10:00AM I received a phone call from a gal named Marge Downing from Terre Haute, Indiana and she wanted to know if I was interested in going to Turkey to work. I told her all that I had heard about Turks was that they ran around on wild horses lopping off heads of people with large scimitar swords. She informed me that it wasn't that bad and she told me that if I would go that they would pay me double the salary I presently made including a lot of fringe benefits. I said, "Oh you're going to pay me $1500 a month tax free?" No, we will pay you $1000 a month; you are only making $500 a month now". After 20 minutes on the phone I said when do we leave. In two weeks I had sold my car, a yellow 59 Imperial hardtop, Made wooden boxes of ¼ "plywood, loaded and ready to ship to Turkey, and had stored my other personal belongings with my Sister, Carol and her husband Ben In Bozeman in a shed behind their house. I left June fourth for Trabzon, Turkey.

June fourth was a hot one in Great Falls 104 degrees when I boarded the DC6 headed for Terre Haute, Indiana. I had to go into Chicago, change planes to Ozark, a commuter line and got into Terre Haute late in the afternoon. It was only 84 degrees there but with humidity to match, the sweat really poured out of me. One day there to get paper work set up and I left for Turkey via Glasgow, Scotland and Frankfurt, Germany. We arrived in

Glasgow at 5:00 a.m. and I don't think I have ever been any colder. It was about 40 degrees with a wind blowing off the ocean made it even colder. From there we went to Frankfurt, changed planes to a Lufthansa and on to Ankara, Turkey. We changed planes again for Turkish Airlines, a twin engine Fokker F-27 I believe they were.

CHAPTER 9

TRABZON, TURKEY

We landed in Trabzon late in the afternoon and when we got on the ground it smelled just like the whole town had crapped their pants and was carrying it around with them.

My Company knew I was coming so they had someone meet me at the airport. I thought to myself, I don't think I can take this place. The company rep helped me check into the best hotel in town and it wouldn't compare to a sailors flop in Boston for 50 cents. The room had a single pull-chain light in the middle of the room, a single bed comparable to a ranch bunkhouse in Montana. The whole place smelled like crap; I went to the bathroom and found out why; two bomb-sight toilets in separate little rooms. One was plugged up and if you pulled the chain a trickle of water ran from the tank up next to the ceiling but not enough to flush anything down. The other toilet room was a little better; when you pulled that chain you might find yourself standing in water on the foot pads. The showers only had warm water in the mornings but at least they worked. I checked in the next morning and then took off to find a place to live. A place to live was tough over there even with someone helping who spoke the language. I started working on the site and would shop for an apartment in the off hours.

After a week or so I found one down close to the beach, owned by Doctor Ozpeker, a ground floor place which had a living room, bedroom, kitchen and a bath area. After getting out of that stinking hotel I thought this was plush and no stink. By now I had gotten accustomed to the town odor. I guess I had acquired the same odor. The bathroom was about 10 feet square with a water tank in one corner, a wood box in the other and the shower was fastened to the wall near the water tank. Near the ceiling was a water tank with a float control to maintain it full and from there gravity fed water into the water tank. At the bottom of the water tank was a fire box which heated the water. My maid would build a fire with just the right amount of wood to have my water just the right temperature so I could shower when I got home from work. If you heated the water too hot you would get a vapor lock in the shower line and no water would come out. To cure this you could turn on both the cold and hot water valves while holding your hand over the shower outlet and water would be forced from the cold water side back up the hot water line to break the vapor lock and voila you have water.

Trabzon was a town of 55,000 people and the US Air force had a little base on top of a hill just north of town which rose right from the seashore up about 700 to a 1000 feet. I don't think it covered more than 10 acres. From there we had the most sophisticated electronic equipment of the time and we spied on Russia.

The Russians were a brazen bunch. Many nights when the moon was bright they would pull the bow of their submarine right up on the sandy beach, pull out all their surveillance equipment and listen and take pictures of us. While they were there we would just shut down our equipment and leave them alone. I have stood up on that hill and waved to them while they took my picture. I am pretty sure I am on KGB film in Russia. The strange thing about American security is that the Russians could take all the pictures they wanted of us and we didn't want an international incident so we did nothing, but if I would have taken a picture of our antenna-array on that hill I would have been on a plane the next day headed for home.

My job was to take care of the electrical facilities around there and I had 22 Turks working for me, all except one, couldn't even fart in English. I immediately enrolled in a night school and I carried a small dictionary in my hip pocket. I started out with four verbs, when, where, what and why. From there I learned how to say when you are going, where you are going, why etc. In 30 days I had a little bit of a working knowledge of their language. Oh yes, the first words I learned were thank you, Good morning, evening etc. After 90 days I thought I was pretty smart and I would stand around down town and visit with the Turks.

One day as I was going to work I stopped at a fruit stand to buy a snack and they had some nice peaches. I knew how to say I am wanting etc. On this day I asked the man running the stand, "bin istiorum bu peach, bu peach etc". The women backed away from the stand and were staring at me. I paid the man and headed on to work. When I got their I asked Ruhi about what had happened and he started laughing uproariously. He said Meester Reechardson, what you were saying was "I am wanting this bastard, this bastard, this bastard etc. When you should have said, Bin istiorum bu sheftali, bu sheftali etc". I never made that mistake again.

Another time I was riding the ferry over to Yalava near Istandul with mostly Americans going back to their base when a Turk with a tray of sandwiches was going around selling them. They were just a bun with a slice of cheese in the middle. He was calling out "Sandoveech elli koroosh, sandoveech elli koroosh" but no one was buying. I bought one for the equivalent of five cents and then told him that Americans no speak Turkish, say it so they understand. Try "son-of-a-beech elli koroosh" and see if you don't sell more. So, away he went yelling "SON-OF-A-BEECH ELLI KOROSH". I motioned for the Yanks to buy some and they did.

I was also getting invited to Turk parties by the Credit Bankasi President, Rifat Kalianjuolu, Ismail Oknas, the director of the British Petroleum and a few more. By six months I was translating for the Air Force and when there was a party down town, the Air Force always made sure I was on the invitation list because I could stand around and translate for them. Most Americans would not learn the language and as a result they hated the place. My thoughts were that if I could speak to people I could better understand their thinking. My final synopsis is that they are a different breed of cat and they never will think like an American. Turkey was 96% Moslem and their religion is like a water pipe, meaning that what light doesn't come into that tube doesn't exist.

I was informed to take a tux if I had one and some good suits when I left the states. I had one tuxedo and by the time I left Turkey I had five. The Turks used to drink Raki and water at parties. Raki is an anisette type white lightning they drink. One night I took two gallons of orange juice to use as mix and from then on the whole town drank Raki and orange juice. The people at these parties were the elite of the town and were well educated. Their women did not wear the veil over their face when they were on the streets and at these parties they wore our western dresses. However on the streets they did wear a scarf over their heads and a woman in Turkey never went on the streets in a short sleeved dress.

The Turk on the street is the one that sets the rules and living according to their Koran, Mohammed passed down several teachings that the Western culture just doesn't understand. One of these being that all men and women must shave all arm pits and posterior parts of their bodies. There is a good reason behind this. When Mohammed was ruling the Church, he found out they had a terrible infestation of body lice, shaving cured this. A Moslem will not eat pork, for a good reason. Many years ago they ate pork in this part of the world but they only have wild hogs there and there are triginosis worms in them.

Many people were getting sick and dying; Mohammed had his doctors check this out and they found these worms in the meat. They were told that if they used much fire under their meat when they cooked and made sure that it was well done they could continue to eat it. They did not do this and they continued to die, so the Hoja of the Church put out the word, NO MORE DOMUS. (Hog). The Jewish people also won't eat pork, probably for the same reason.

While I was there I would take a $200 draw each month and on this I could live like a king. On the fruit stands downtown fresh fruit would be about two and 1/2 cents a kilo. That's 2.2 lbs, US, lamb 60 cents a kilo, beef, which was water buffalo, 60 cents a kilo for Loin cuts. My apartment $25 a month but I had to furnish my own oil for my heating stove. I paid my maid $10 a month and she was being overpaid $2.50 a month, which the Turks didn't like it because I was creating inflation for them. I explained that Americans were hard to work for and we demanded more than the Turks and that appeased them.

I felt sorry for my Sonianna so I would buy things for her from the mail order catalogs in the PX and I always kept her supplied with Vicks which she used on her arthritic joints. She was a 79 year old white Russian who didn't look a day over 50. One day, I was sitting upstairs on the 3rd floor having tea with my Landlord, Dr Ozpeker, when she came up there with a load of wood in her apron. She set it down in the middle of the floor exclaiming that she just wasn't the woman she used to be. I told her that I would help carry up heavy loads like that. To that she replied, "NO NO that's my job". I went over and lifted the apron full of wood and I swear it must have weighed 150 pounds.

These people are extremely strong. I have seen a Hamal pick up a basket full of melons that possibly weighed 250 lbs or better and they would walk up a 20% grade in the street. A Hamal is a man that carries things for people rather than use a truck, which are in scarce supply. When I would go shopping I would hire a hamal with a basket to follow us around and as we bought things we would toss them in his basket. We would pay 10 to 40 cents usually. If we kept him most of the day we would buy him lunch but if we ate in a restaurant he would eat outside on the street. Also Turks did not want us to feed them too good or pay them more than the Natives would because we would be breaking down conditions for the locals.

Also in town they had a man who would lift diesel engines out of trucks when they had to be changed. He would stand on the fenders with a harness around his shoulders and he would lift then they would block the engine and he would get another bite on the harness and lift it some more. A simple tripod with a block and tackle would have done the job much easier. Turks use very primitive ways to get the job done.

For building their roads you will see caterpillar graders and other heavy equipment which I am sure was donated by the Americans, but the private enterprise did not have such luxuries.

On the shipping docks I have seen whole ship loads of wheat piled on the docks with tarps over it. Rats and mice ate their share and when it rained I am sure mildew ruined a good part of it. It would have been so simple to have built some metal granaries for it.

I have never seen any machinery on the local farms so I assume they plant their grains by hand. They harvest it with a crude looking scythe and the women and children do most of the work. The children and sometimes the women carry this to an area and throw it on the ground. The master of the house (the man) has a platform of boards nailed together, maybe six to eight foot square. This is pulled by a water buffalo and the man sits on a straight backed kitchen chair driving the water buffalo in circles grinding the grain into the ground.

He will then move to a new spot and the women will scoop up the dirt and grain into a large wicker type basket and toss it into the air just enough to let the wind catch the dust and chaf and blow it away and leaving the grain in the basket.

Women would cut corn stalks in the fields and would load a bundle of maybe 150 to 200 pounds on their backs and walk home. We would be walking behind them with our cameras strapped from our necks. One guy would stop to tie his shoe lace and the rest of us would shoot pictures from the waist. Sometimes we would miss but for the most part we got some excellent pictures of the working people.

I must say the Americans are too trusting when it comes to other nations. I have sat and discussed politics, cultures, women and many other topics. They have developed a different culture through the many centuries and in my opinion they will never see eye to eye with our reasoning.

During this time when they are working in the fields their small babies will lie in a bassinet unprotected out in the hot sun. I am sure that many of them end up with brain damage. You want to go teach them a better way but their Moslem beliefs are ingrained so deeply that they do not want to change one way of their past.

One day I saw them excavating a trench in town. I stopped to see what was going on. They were repairing the sewer line and there about 8 feet down were men laying flat stones in the bottom of the ditch, then more flat stones set vertically to them, some sand dirt to hold them in place, then the final flat stones were laid on top and that was the main sewer line. This sewer line ran down to the beach and into the sea. I couldn't believe it.

During a visit to Germany in 1962 I bought Adenauer's old 1956 Cadillac for $750, with only 25,000 miles on it, which I thought I would resell to a rich cotton farmer in southern Turkey and make some money. Between the time I left and got back to Turkey they had changed their laws. No vehicle over six cylinders, over 1500 kilos, and so many centimeters in length could not be imported anymore. I was over on all counts so I just put it on my passport and drove it while I was there. Greece and Iran had also changed their laws.

It was a beautiful car in mint condition so it impressed a lot of people. I tried to give it to the Prime Minister in Ankara but he declined saying that they were a very poor country and if he rode around in a car like that it would not look good in the eyes of the people. So I was known as the CAUDEELAK MAAN in Trabzon. We drove around the countryside and saw lots of nice things. I now know how the Elizabeth Taylors feel. People just wanted to touch you and they would stare because for the most part they had never seen such a rich person.

They only refine regular 80 octane gas there and this car was supposed to use ETHEL, which was the super grade of the time. It didn't run too well on 80 octane so I would buy mothballs at the PX and I would add one to the gallon when I filled the tank. That cured all problems with the fuel.

During this time when they are working in the fields their small babies will lie in a bassinet, unprotected, out in the hot sun. I am sure that many of them end up with brain damage. You want to go teach them a better way but their Moslem beliefs are ingrained so deeply that they do not want to change one bit of their past.

While I was there they had a hepatitis outbreak and I think they had 5000 cases in a town of 55,000 people. We did some investigating and found that the river was contaminated and our wells were also right by the Turks wells down by the river. We took extra precaution and treated ours with a heavy dose of chlorine. I also told the Turks doing this job for us to also dump a dose in the Turk wells. A few hours later when people opened their faucets down town, almost a muddy mess came out and according the them the smell was terrible. That awful smell to them was chlorine. Within a short time they had all the fire hydrants open and was flushing the lines and they were mad as hell.

What had happened was that the lines were old wooden lines with wire windings on the outside. Over the years, algae had built up inside the lines and when that chlorine went through, it killed the algae, which came loose from the walls of the pipes. We finally had to admit that the Americans had put the chlorine in the well and it came back to me who was in charge. For that I was severely reprimanded and they wanted me fired. One thing was accomplished though, was that the outbreak of hepatitis was over.

During the time of the outbreak we had a small party at our house and one of the town doctors and his wife were there. She wanted a drink of water and she would not drink our chlorinated water which we kept in a plastic jug.

CHAPTER 10

RECREATION IN TURKEY

*T*here weren't any lack of things to do. The military had things to keep them busy, such as baseball, tennis, pool tables, ping pong, and sightseeing trips. The civilians didn't get involved much in the on-base sports but we did go on a bus tour South of Trabzon to a little town that had some ancient museums with mummies in them and some burial crypts that had been carved out of solid rock high up on a hill at the edge of town. These crypts were about 15 feet high and several feet into the rock. It was a steaming hot day and I couldn't get anyone to go with me to climb the hill up on the mountain. We did see a lot of things around town and some ancient dwellings that had been built many years before.

On occasions we would rent a taxi, which didn't cost much and take a trip out of town. We would always rent a taxi and driver because if we as Americans ever got into an accident, there would be a good chance that we would be found at fault and you might never get out of the Country.

One day Ingrid and I, and I will explain her later, took a cab and went out into the country. We stopped along the road where five dirty little urchins, covered with dust and dirt, were playing by an old shack. We gave each of them a lira coin which was about 10 cents, and some candy. Then the father comes out from the back of the house and we visited with him. We asked him how many children he had and his answer was 18. Ingrid then asked him how many wives he had to which he answered three. Then she opened a can of worms. She asked where the wives and older children were. He said they are all out in the fields working and the youngest wife was just over the knoll watching us and she was about eight months pregnant he told us. So he told us. She was crouched on the ground and we could just see her head and shoulders. He would not allow her to come up and meet us.

The second can of worms Ingrid then opened was when she suggested that he should be out in the fields working and the mothers should be home taking care of the children.

He said, "You Americans, you are always running around the world trying to tell everyone else how to live; now you look at it from my point of view, I get up in the morning and get everybody out to work; I then go to Chay House, (that's their tea house) I have tea bread and cheese, I then visit with my friends, After lunch we have a little Raki, we play cards and talk. Now, are you going to tell me you can improve on that?" He may be right, all my wives always made me do the work.

We also had six boats ranging from 14 to 20 feet that sat down at the harbor. They were not locked up and the keys were just tucked up under the dash. As civilians we had to sign out for these when we wanted to use them but they never refused us. We would got out in the Black Sea about a mile, so that we were in clean water and we would fish or just go swimming.

CHAPTER 11

ESPIONAGE

$\mathcal{I}$n 1960 an RB-47 Surveillance Plane was flying over eastern Turkey and was lured over the border into Russia and shot down with a missile. To accomplish this they would block out our navigational signals and superimpose their signal. If our pilots were not careful they could easily fly over the border into Russia and blooey, up would come a missile, down one plane and a charge of spying would hit the airways, an International incident.

In 1962 our C-130 was bringing in supplies and mail and this is what the pilot related to us after he got on the ground, He kept calling Trabzon Radio to request landing instructions but no answer. After numerous times, he waited a few minutes and tried again, and in perfect English came the reply, "Yes, Air Force C130 (a number I will use because I don't remember his flight number), this is Trabzon radio, your about 50 miles out, we have you locked on radar, we will give you landing instructions when you get closer". The pilot flew about 15 seconds more and then a light bulb came on and he realized Trabzon doesn't have radar. He said he damn near did a shandell in that big son-of-a-bitch getting it turned around. He said he turned it north which he knew would take him out over the Black Sea. We had an inversion layer of clouds that usually hung over the coastal area at about a 500 foot ceiling and the mountains rise rapidly from the coast so they had to be careful not to let down too soon when coming in because the runway was right on the beach. We did not have the best navigational equipment for the airport so caution was of importance.

After he had let the plane down till he could see water, they then headed towards land and followed it up to the airport on the radio beam. Had he flown another minute he would have been over the Russian border and we very likely would have had another International incident and all of our mail and weekly supplies would have gone up in smoke.

I developed a pretty close friendship with Allen R. Johnson, the base photographer and he taught me how to use a dark room. They used a tremendous amount of Polaroid film in the operations building and when it became one day out of date, they could not use it; so he would give it to us guys for our personal use. Sometime we would amuse the Turks downtown with this magic. You never take a picture of a Turk without his permission and at no time do you photograph their women. We would ask a Turk if we could take his picture and then we would give them the finished product. They had never seen Polaroid Cameras so this was pure magic to them.

Also Allen would supply us with all the black and white film we wanted in cans of 100 feet. We would load it into cassettes and shoot all the pictures we wanted. Groups of us would take walks in the country and since I had a 350 MM telephoto lens I would set up a tripod, and while we were visiting I would swing it around and take pictures of women working in the fields.

When Kennedy was visiting Berlin, the Air Force flew Johnson's wife from San Antonio, Texas to Berlin and set her up in a nice hotel and Allen was flown out of Trabzon in the middle of the night to Berlin as one of the official photographers. They had been in Berlin two days when the Russian radio station which played a lot of good American music, came on with the announcement, "Welcome to Berlin, Sergeant Allen R. Johnson, serial number etc. etc. We wish you and your wife a pleasant stay in Berlin." I didn't even know that he had left Trabzon. Those Russians had a damned good espionage system. I feel that someone within our own organization had to have tipped off the Russians that he was going to Berlin.

Trabzon was also the last station to have communication with Gary Power before his U-2 was shot down over Russia in 1960. I had a two martini and a three hour lunch with him later when I worked for Lockheed in 1969. Poor devil, took a job later flying a traffic chopper in LA and it went down killing him. He was 48 or 49 years old at that time.

CHAPTER 12

ALL THE WOMEN I LOVED

Catherine #1

1 suppose at this time I should bow my head in shame and admit the history of my wives. At this time I was working in engine service as a fireman for the Milwaukee Railroad.

I was 23 years old, horney, like most young men and I met this tall blond Missourian in town and one thing led to another. I married her about six months later and we lived together for about one year. She was a real renegade, she was screwing another fireman who worked on the railroad and who knows who else. We had a stormy marriage and within a year while I was out on a run she loaded up the car and left for Missouri. I decided that I wasn't going to let that wench get away with my new Pontiac so I got a pass and took off on the train for Missouri. In the meantime she was on her way back to Montana with a deputy Sheriff. Red Pryor had spent most of one night with our local telephone operator calling along the route that the train took and they located me just getting on a bus in Otumwa, Iowa. I rushed on down to Edina, Missouri and convinced her brother to tell me where the car was hidden. I got into the garage and backed it out and roared out of town. The tank registered empty so I stopped about 12 miles out and filled it with gas, checked the oil and it didn't even touch the bottom of the dipstick. The station owner dumped the oil and refilled it and I took off. I zeroed the speedometer and 1399 miles and 23 hours later I pulled into Three Forks. My friend Red Pryor informed me that she was back in town with a deputy Sheriff from Missouri and they had been looking for my truck. They wanted to hook onto the trailer and haul it off also. Red had hot-wired my truck and had hid it in a local construction company's garage. I put the car in my neighbor's garage.

All night long they were hanging around the bars and would drive by the trailer and shine their spotlight in the windows. I had to make a run on the railroad so my sister Vivian slept in the house while I was gone to keep them out of the trailer. This went on for about 4 days and one night I called Peck Bacon's house, our deputy sheriff, and asked him to make them stop shining the spot light on the house, that it was also shining into my neighbor's bedroom windows. He went down to Fred's Place, a bar and grill, and informed them to stop it. They kind of sneered at him and he left. He called me back and reminded me not to do anything that would get me in trouble. About 2 a.m. that night they showed up again with the lights on. I took my 22 rifle and cut a small hole in the screen and stuck it out the window. They came back around again and I fired. I hit that spotlight dead center and a little blue smoke came up and the light was out. Two hours later that boy left town.

When I made that trip back from Missouri with the car running 90 to 100 miles per hour all the way, it got rather a hard run. When I arrived in Three Forks, I ran it right into a garage and shut it down. That was a mistake; I should have let it idle for a while to cool down because the valves were probably red hot and they warped. The next morning I went out to start the car and it would barely run. Anyway I had to give her the car, and some more, for her settlement in the divorce as set forth by our Illustrious Judge Lesley in Bozeman. Seth Bohart my attorney asked that the case be transferred to another judge because we felt that Judge Lesley was biased in his opinion. The case finally came up in Helena under another judge and he couldn't believe Lesley's opinion. I ended up giving her the car, no alimony, nor cash. I'll bet she had a hell of a time keeping it running all the way back to Missouri.

Twenty-four years later, Kay's brother Jim died, who was a rancher near Radersburg. She came out for the funeral and she called my sister Carol to find out where I lived and she came to Anaconda to see me. She now owned a bar in Iowa and was doing OK. We had a short visit and she wanted to know if we could get back together. The answer was no way. By this time I had gone through two more women and I had a nice refrigeration business going. I did feel very sorry for her because her son, Ray who was three years old when I married her, was a nice sweet little boy. He had gone to Viet Nam and was killed in action when he was just 18.

Wife# 2, Jean

I dated girls from Bozeman, Whitehall and a few local gals while living in Three Forks.

One day a new girl came in from Lima, Montana and went to work for LaVeeta, who owned the restaurant where I ate most of my meals. Jean's former husband was a gambler who owned a bar in Lima, Montana and from what Jean told me later was that he made many payments to the police chiefs and sheriffs all the way from Lima to Butte so he could run his card games. Gambling at this time was illegal in Montana.

Within a couple of weeks he was found dead on the old road to Trident with his head propped up on a pillow behind the tail pipe of his car and the engine running. However a few things didn't ring out right, his shoe was found 20 feet from the car and our local law officer didn't think his head was close enough to the tail pipe to have killed him. Everyone knew he was a gambler and they figured that someone had done him in, probably a loser at one of his games.

One of the things she told me later was that he would take his new decks of cards home, and with a razor blade shave under the cellophane seals, remove the cards and mark them, then reseal them. When they would have a game and a guy was losing too much he might ask for a new deck. No problem, he would whip out a new deck and break the cellophane seals and a new deck were in the game. What the victim didn't know was that the cards were already marked. If a guy was a regular, he might let him win a night or two so that he didn't lose him from the crowd. Jean said that he could deal you just about any hand he wanted and he was so good that he never got caught.

After a month or so I asked her if she wanted to go to a movie in Bozeman and she accepted. On our way home we made a stop in a secluded area and had a little fun. The very next night after I had gone to bed there was a knock on my bedroom door of the trailer. When I opened it, in stepped Jean. This became an every night visit and after three weeks I had to go to Lewistown to work on the Branch lines of the Milwaukee, which were all steam engines. She begged me to take her along and I said, "No, I couldn't." Then she said just let me ride up there with you and I'll catch a bus back to Three Forks. I finally agreed to that and she went with me for the 160-mile ride.

In Lewistown I checked into a trailer park and within an hour or so I was all hooked up and leveled. She just wanted to stay for a few days and that became a month and since this was the most passionate woman I had ever known, I let her stay. A couple of months later I had to move on to Great Falls in able to keep working. After several months I sold my trailer and moved into a small house owned by a retired schoolteacher. Jean and I ended up getting married.

Jean was the best companion a man could have and the best lover this side of heaven. If I went fishing or hunting she was not to be left behind. I bought her a 270 rifle and she always got her deer and one elk while we were married. One time we were going fishing up near Augusta and in fording a creek we hit a rock and knocked a tie-rod off the truck. This was early in the morning and I had to cut trees down and literally build a bridge under the front of the truck, anchor the tie-rod and at 4:00 P.M. we finally got backed out of that mess. After we got out there was a nice little patch of grass right close so we pitched the tent, built a fire and broke out the bottle of whiskey and had two or three good drinks. Mind you, that mountain water was ice cold and we were chilled to the bone even though we had hip boots on, so the whiskey tasted mighty fine. She was down in that water right with me working to jack up the front of the vehicle. I loosened the drain plug on the crankcase when we got out and let it drain the water out and the next morning we packed up and went back to Great Falls at about 35 miles per hour. I had to have the differential and transmission drained and refilled, all the bearings packed and the old truck ran for some time.

Jean was a beautiful dancer and was dressed in the finest when we went to a formal ball.

One problem after five years of marriage, I had slowed down to about three or four times a week rather than the daily or multi-daily episodes. The Milwaukee Railroad was going downhill fast so I had taken a job with the Montana Power Company. I was trying to give her more than I could afford and by the time we made our monthly payments it left nothing for entertainment. She went to work for a dress shop down town and within a short time; an old bitch at the store convinced her that they should stop after work for a drink. It was getting later each day when she would get home and finally one night when a guy brought her home at 3:00 in the morning, I was waiting. She even admitted that she couldn't keep her pants up. Another divorce. Another wife who six months later came around and begged me to come back. I had to sell the new house furnished and I gave Jean our little Karman Ghia as her share of the settlement. I had bought her an electric organ because she wanted to learn to play one and I was able to sell it for what I owed on it. I was the only one that learned to play it to any extent. During the time she worked she never made one single payment on anything.

Within a year I was offered a job in Eastern Turkey so I was gone. She married a Sergeant out at the Airbase and in 1999 I met her brother Pete at a little town out in the desert by Quartzite, Arizona. She had died of breast cancer in 1987 in Virginia Beach, Virginia. She was 64 years old at that time. I have spoken with her sister Shirley as late as 2003 and she said the last year of her life was a complete hell for her with a lot of intense pain. She had made several trips back there from Montana to help care for her. At her death she was married to a sailor and they had stayed together all the years after she left Great Falls. I would suspect that his being out to sea a good portion of the time, he didn't know what went on at home. I don't know what happened to the Sergeant that was a previous account.

Wife #3 Ingrid

While working in Turkey, I made several trips to Europe and there I met Ingrid, a beautiful blond German girl. I brought her to Turkey and after six months we returned to Koln and got married. After a couple of years there and going to all those formal parties with numerous handsome men, who were without their wives, she weakened and had an affair with at least one of them. When I found out about this, I quit my job and returned to the US. I did not want another divorce so I didn't divorce her. In March of '64, I had checked out with my Company and we decided to make a pilgrimage through the Holy Land. When I found out about her affair, things had cooled off and we had not had sex for six weeks. That night in Ankara we went out to a stage show, dinner, champagne and all. When we got back to the hotel, we made love.

We met another couple there that had a VW Beetle and they also were going to the Holy Land. They invited us to join them and the next day we all left. The next day we made it all the way to the Mediterranean Sea but it was 9:00 PM. We were traveling along the sea coast and saw a bunch of cabins. We found the owner and for $1.00 each we rented two cabins for the night. They were furnished with two army cots each and nothing else. At this point we didn't care but we were all sweaty and wanted a bath but no soap. Ingrid found a small bottle of Palmolive dish soap in her bag so we decided to use that. No one had a swim suit but since it was blacker than a stack of black cats we decided to go nude. Out in the water we each took a short squeeze of soap and lathered up. We swam out in the sea and then standing waste deep in water we tried to rinse off. We would end up with a pile of foam around us, move to a clean spot of water and another pile of foam. It seemed there was no end to this so we swam around some and got out. We all went to bed and the next morning we headed for Syria.

We all decided to go to Aleppo, Syria because they had heard there were some fantastic ruins there. We checked into the best hotel in town and it was a first class hotel. Our room was a large room with a sitting area and a couch, a bath that was nearly as large as the main room and the carpets were a very deep pile, medium blue and absolutely beautiful. Cost, in U.S. equivalent, $6.24 a day including a full breakfast. Almost all taxis were Mercedes Benz and the cost to go across town, 25 cents. The population was about 100,000 at that time and the people were very gracious and friendly. The other couple left in two days but we stayed a week and saw it all. The Citadel had a moat around it and is still standing. In the middle were many rooms, most of them displayed some fine marble work. There were some water and sewer lines that looked similar to the clay material that we use in the U.S. They had steam-bath rooms as well as bathing areas. After a week there we decided to go to Beirut, Lebanon and were advised by the hotel to take a taxi. I don't remember but it must have been close to 160 miles and we shared the cab with another Lebanese couple. The cost was $6.25 for Ingrid and me.

By this time Ingrid was getting sick every evening around 6:00PM. What we didn't know at the time was that it was morning sickness but coming on in the evening due to her being pregnant.

We arrived in Beirut in the late afternoon and went to the Phoenician Hotel and they wanted $120 a night for a room. We then went to the Pan Am hotel and they wanted $105 a night. This was kind of a cold water shock after having such a nice hotel in Syria for so little and then gets hit with this. I came out and got into our taxi and asked him if he could take us to a part of town where they might have some apartments. We didn't go half mile before he came to an apartment hotel with a vacancy sign. I went in and met the landlady and asked her if we could rent an apartment for a week but she informed that she only rented by the month. Upon questioning her, she informed that the rent for a month was $105. I told her I would be willing to pay a premium if she could rent us a unit for just a week. She thought a moment and said that she would have to have at least $30 for a week. I jumped on that but what we didn't know was that the room or apartment had a living room, small kitchenette, and a nice bedroom plus it came with maid service. The next morning at about 6:30 a.m., I heard a little noise out in the kitchen and when I checked, there was the maid and she wanted to know if I wanted coffee. This was quite a shock to me but I said thanks very much. After that the coffee was ready each morning by 7:00AM and the room was spruced up each day and all the dishes washed. I guess you know that maid got a $10.00 tip when we left and if you think that is cheap of me, remember that was a month's wages for maid service during these times.

We thoroughly enjoyed Beirut and we made side trips to Balbek, the beaches, museums etc.

At this time the country was about 25 percent Christian and 75 % Muslim and everybody cohabitated very nicely. It is such a shame that today they have virtually destroyed the town because the Muslims want total control.

After seven days we left by taxi again and went down through Jordan and into Jerusalem and found that the town was still packed with visitors and there weren't any rooms available. Our Fire Chief at Trabzon, Turkey had a daughter that had married the son of Canavatti, an owner of five gift shop stores in Jerusalem. Our taxi driver knew where to find him and we went to his shop and because we were friends of his son-in-law, he left his store with the help and he took us to Bethlehem to the Bethlehem Ladies Club. This was like a small hotel but it had only three rooms that they rented. There was one room left and we got it for $2.75 a night. The other two rooms were rented to a doctor and his nurse who were from Germany and they were there to treat and study eye diseases. What luck, we could have been sleeping in a manger also because this was the last room in town as far as we knew.

We visited several times with Canavatti and he was making a small fortune selling gifts to the tourists. As an example, one day I was standing around in his store and an American couple came in and they were emanating of wealth. They were interested in a pair of parakeet birds carved from green jade with a price tag of $640 on them. Finally the American told Canavatti that he was interested in them but he would not pay a dime more than $500 for them. Canavatti wrapped them up in a hurry and later told me that if the guy would have offered him $300 he could have had them. They were carved in China and he had paid $60.00 for the pair.

Canavatti sold me 2 two Masonic commemorative boxes made of olive-wood with a gavel and a keystone for $35.00. The keystone and gavel were made of limestone from the mines under the city. These mines had been closed down for some time but we were told that the only source of this limestone was from these mines and that is where King Solomon's temple had also gotten the stone when it was constructed. It is believed by some that King Solomon's Temple was built about where the Dome of the Rock Muslim temple stands today.

We toured around the Middle East and after a few weeks we crossed back over into Israel and headed to Haifa. We booked passage on the Shalom Liner for Marseille, France which took several days for that cruise. We picked up a newspaper in Genoa, Italy and found an ad for a 1962 VW for sale for $500; this was in 1964. We got off the boat and took a train to Munich,

Germany and found the owner. It had a sliding sun roof and low mileage but it had a bad valve in the engine. I bought it anyway and we limped up to Koln, Germany where I went to a VW dealer and had a new engine installed for $150.

We arrived in Koln at about 3:50 PM at the VW dealer. I explained to the service manager that we had a burnt valve and that I wanted a new engine installed. He argued with me that it would be much cheaper to just repair the engine but I kept insisting on a new motor. He finally turned to two apprentice mechanics and said, "I have ein dumbkopf American who wants a new motor, give it to him." These two kids were 15 and 16 years old and 46 minutes later I drove out with the new engine for $150. When I paid the bill I explained to the service manager in German the reason I wanted a new engine. We were going to America and would be selling the car as soon as we finished our vacation and if I advertised a car with a repaired engine it would not sell as fast as one advertised with a new engine and probably for less money. His face turned red but he came back with, "you Americans always thinking of money." I drove the car 10,000 miles and sold it in Great Falls, Montana in three days and made $300 profit.

I borrowed my sister and bother-in-law's camp trailer and drove up the Gallatin canyon and went fishing for six months. We really got our fill of nice rainbow trout.

During the day I typed out 100 copies of my resume and sent them out. I got back four interested replies but no firm offers. I was making so much money working overseas that the stateside companies were shy of me. I finally got on a phone and called Bob Carlson in Germany whom I had only met on a flight from Ankara, Turkey to Frankfurt. He remembered me and said get your butt on a plane and there is a job waiting for you when you get here.

Ingrid was now about six months pregnant, but we packed our bags and took off.

When we got to Frankfurt he set me up with a crew and we went to Linderhofe, Germany and started building a missile site. These were the same sites that Reagan gave up in 1988 when he met with Gorbeshev. By this time they were 20 years old and obsolete so it was a very good move on America's part. I worked on some in Holland, one at Giesen, Germany, Villingen, Germany and Finalle Legura, Italy. Finalle Legura to me is the prettiest little town in Italy. It sits on the northern Riviera between Genoa and San Reimo and I traveled through almost all of the towns in Italy and I rated it number one. We paid $64 a month for the apartment, furnished down to the linens and silverware. Geuseppi Puppo was the best landlord in the area. Every week he would bring us some fruits or vegetables from his farm and we would find them on the dining table when we got home in the evening.

While I was at Finale Legura on the Northern Riviera of Italy, I thought this was the most beautiful little town in the Country. The promenade along the beach down town had potted flower pots hanging on a rack around the palm trees and they had swings and chairs along the entire street for you to sit and enjoy the beauty. Also the restaurants along the street were busy serving, coffee, ice cream etc to the tourists.

I ran into a little trouble there right off the start when I arrived there. We were running a little behind schedule and I wasn't getting enough work out of the men. The reason being that they were all single and they would go to the Club Boncardo or the 21 Club and pick up a pale faced young Swedish or German girl and move them into their Villa. She would have three to four weeks of fun and frolic with the guys and it saved her money. In a month she had a tan like a model and she would go home. They would pick up another new arrival with pale skin and repeat it all over.

Finally I called them all in and laid the law down. If a man should come to work with the smell of liquor on his breath and hung over he would catch the next plane back to Frankfurt.

Furthermore I informed them that we would be working twelve hour days. Then after that rock dropped I said but that will be three days one week and then they would have four days off; the following week we would work three twelve hour days and one eight hour day and then they would have three days off. This worked and we caught up on schedule and they loved that. I also liked it because we would take our car and tour around the country or even go over to France.

Our Baby was born on December 12, 1964 before we left Linderhofe, Germany. We named him Dean because we didn't think there was a nickname for Dean. When we got to Italy Dean was a sweet looking baby and the first day that we wheeled him down town in his buggy; the Italian women would stop to admire him and they asked what his name was. When we told them it was Dean, they ooed and awed and said in Italian that's Dino. It stuck and even today I catch myself calling him Dino at times.

On this job I fractured a vertebra and spent six weeks in a body cast. What a horrible thing, I could not go out in the ocean and dive by the hour, or lie in the sun. I finally ended up back at Linderhofe and the job was winding down. My Company let everybody go but they sold my contract to the Army and I was used as their trouble shooter when things would go wrong. I also trained the GI's that were to take over the sites. Thinking that I was going home I had bought a new Mercedes diesel ($2900) but then I had to stay. I traveled all over Europe correcting problems and at the end of six months I had put 30,000 miles on my new car. We finally turned over all the sites to the U.S. Army and I headed home.

We drove our car to Rotterdam, Holland, turned it over to a Norwegian shipping company and had it shipped to New York. Then we went back to Köln, Germany to visit with Ingrid's parents and from there went to Brussels, Belgium, caught Loftleider Air Lines, which is the Icelandic Airlines and were on our way home.

We still had one little problem to overcome; Loftleider used DC 6 planes and out of

Glasgow, Scotland past the point of no-return, I noticed a little trail of smoke coming from the outboard starboard engine. I buzzed the stewardess and tried to get her to bend over close to me so I could tell her about the smoke. She was half nasty and finally I stood up took her by the arm and told her that if I yelled out loud enough for her to hear me to explain the problem the whole plane would be in an uproar. Finally I held her arm and said get your butt up there to the Captain and tell him he better be checking this engine. She did and in about two minutes he cut the engine and feathered the prop. Now I began to get concerned because we had 108 people aboard [not an empty seat] so I figured they would start dumping luggage. The other three engines were wound up to take-off RPM. Anyway we made it to Reykjavik and set down at 11:30PM. It was still enough daylight to take pictures so I took a few. Before we got off the plane the Captain announced that if anyone wanted to stay overnight and leave the next evening at 11:00 p.m., we could have drinks in the bar, free hotel and meals and a tour of the Island the next day. Such a deal I couldn't pass it up. They have enough thermal hot springs on the Island that they furnish all the hot water for heating on the entire island. The other thing that amazed me was the number of earthquake fault-lines. They are everywhere and it was a very interesting day.

Upon arrival in New York the following day we stayed at a friend's apartment on East 63rd until our car arrived. This friend was on a Round-the-world trip that we met on a Pan Am flight previously and she offered us her apartment. She was a proof-reader for a publishing company. Now I know why I live in Montana. I opened the window to let in some fresh air and there was an inch of soot on the window sill. I took a dust pan and cleaned it all up. I left the window open about four inches and the next morning there was another quarter inch of soot on the sill. After that we used the air conditioner and left the windows closed.

While we were waiting for the car to arrive we went to the World's Fair of 1964. I was fascinated by that and we really enjoyed it.

We then went down to pick up our car and I had another run-in with the Longshoremen; they wanted $25 just to connect up the battery cable. I checked the foot locker in the trunk and found that a Blaupunkt radio was missing. You couldn't prove anything but they got real nasty with me and I finally went into talk to the Policeman and he brought out the head Honcho for the Longshoremen. He told them very curtly that they should give me my car. They did and we got the hell out of there. My opinion of Longshoremen is about the same as the German Gestapo in the forties.

Wife 4 Priscilla

*A*fter Ingrid and I parted company and I was established in Anaconda, Montana about two or three years had passed. Now that I was back in Montana I became active again in the Masonic Lodge and the Shrine in Butte.

I was familiar with the organization called Parents without Partners from LA so I got busy and started a new branch up there. There I met a nice lady, a little younger that I and we dated regularly. She had two sons, one 14 and the other 16. The younger one Bruce was a little renegade and lived with his Uncle in Dillon most of the time. David was a straight A student and wanted to be a history teacher but he had some rather weird habits. When he would eat he would have his head down over his plate and would just shovel the food into his mouth. It reminded me of what I had seen retarded people do. I mentioned his table manners to Priscilla but she wasn't about to accept any criticism of her son. Bruce called up one time and was going to quit school and join a monastery. His mother hit the ceiling and when she came down, I said let me handle this. She did and I had him come up to Anaconda to meet the local priest who could help in this matter. The priest didn't want to have anything to do with me because I was a protestant but I convinced him to help since Bruce was raised a Catholic. We went down to the church and laid out the problem. The priest informed Bruce that you had to have a good education to become a Monk and that he should finish school and keep his grades up and then come back and talk. I knew this was only a teenager's pipe dream so we left. Bruce only had four months to go before he would graduate from high school so I convinced him to stick it out. I made a few trips to Dillon to see him and I suggested that he join the Military after he got out of school. He did just that and he ended up In Italy and finally married an Italian girl and they had two children the last time I heard from him. He ended up back in the states in Kentucky and we corresponded regularly. Finally for some reason we lost contact. I have gotten on the internet to try to find him but always came up blank. We maintained communications for 10 or 15 years. His mother, Priscilla had an attorney send me a letter a few years later while I was in San Diego to see if I would sign a document so that she might return to the name Richardson for her last name.

She is another one that told me she made a terrible mistake by walking out on me. She didn't get along with Dean very well but I convinced Dean to just do what she asked and everything would be OK. She was a heavy smoker but we learned to live with that and we had some good times together. She had a 17 foot camp trailer and we would go to the lakes on weekends, fish and ride the Hondas.

One time she and I were in Butte and decided to go to Bozeman to have lunch with my sister Leva. She said it's too late we can't make it by lunch time. I said that's OK I know where she has lunch and we will just go there. It was 11:00 AM on the dot when we pulled onto the freeway at the Harrison on ramp in my little Mazda rotary engine car. As we came off the Butte Mountain and headed across the Whitehall flats I let it go and we pegged the speedometer at 135 MPH. It seemed very light and I didn't think I would even want to get caught with a 10 mile per hour cross wind so I dropped it back to 120. At 11:46 we pulled off at the seventh street off ramp in Bozeman, 46 minutes to go 87 miles. Not bad crossing the Continental Divide and another range out of Whitehall. Leva worked at Penny's so we took her to lunch at 12:00 noon.

On another occasion we were out deer hunting and she was driving her Jeep Waggoner four wheel drive up a rather steep hill and the tire lanes were snow packed. Off to the right was about a 45 degree slope and a good 30 feet before any trees would catch you should it slip off. I asked her if I could take it up that hill and she replied, "I am a good driver, I'll do it". About half way up the car spun out and she set the brakes but it kept sliding back and finally stopped on the right edge of that bank. She very calmly put it in park, set the foot brake and said, "It's your turn to drive." We exchanged places and I got it to move upward on that edge by staying out of the slick paths, then very carefully once it was rolling, I got back across the slick paths and hugged the bluff side in the loose snow until we got over the top. We got our deer that day.

Priscilla and I had a lot of fun but one day over practically nothing she got angry and just left. I tried to convince her to come back but no way.

Another gal that said within six months that leaving me was the worst decision she could have made.

Wife 5, Betty

Dean and I were headed for San Filipe, Mexico and we stopped in L.A. so he could visit his mother on the way home. She had remarried and had a nice business going with her restaurant in Tarzana. She had a friend named Betty that she thought would make an excellent mate for me. She was a good looking brunette and I fell for that. After a whirlwind courtship and her flying to Montana and me vice-versa, we got married. I moved her to Montana and she had transferred to Butte with the Telephone Company. Four stormy months later she was going to work one morning and there was some frost on the road, and she thought you could still drive 70 miles per hours. She was driving my Mazda and flipped it over on an overpass near Butte. It landed on its top and when she released her seat belt she came down on her head, kinked her neck a little but nothing serious, thank God. I got a call from the local Police so I headed out there. She was complaining because she snagged her nylons. I retorted that I think I could buy her new nylons cheaper than I could replace the car. When I got the mess cleaned up and had Micky Nazzer haul my car home and Betty back in a warm house, she let loose and told me to get her out of this damned cold hell hole and back to L.A. I loaded her stuff in a U haul and returned her to L.A. Then the calls started the crying and I know we can make it. Around this time Urban Renewal had informed the people of Anaconda that they were going to build a mall in town and of course my building was in the middle of the area that they wanted to demolish. Everybody started hiring lawyers and was suing; I took a different approach. I took the director to lunch a few times and discussed the situation. I ended up getting about $10,000 more than the others. No lawyer's fees either.

Betty kept calling and would even fly up to Anaconda to see me and convinced me that her ways had changed if only she could live in California. I sold out and moved to San Diego and started a new refrigeration business. I wanted to take the cash I had and buy a 10 unit apartment house than I had found in a good location and live in one unit and be my own manager. Betty was not going to have anything to do with it. She wanted a nice home so we bought a nice three bedroom home on Blue Lake Drive in San Carlos.. This lasted five months and she was constantly complaining, however I had no rights to complain. As an example, she wanted to run around the house in her pantyhose and bra. My son Dean was 10 years old and I suggested that this was not any way to raise a 10 year old boy. The pubic hair showed clearly through the pantyhose and her large breasts left plenty exposed.. One thing led to another and she filed for Divorce and was going to clean me good. When we went to court in San Diego, the judge took one look at her and told her she had two weeks to get out of my house and not to take one stick of anything that she didn't bring in. To show you how vengeful some people can be, she moved a day earlier than what she told me, so I was not there. She took all her potted plants and threw the dirt all over the carpeting. I was so happy to get rid of her, Dean and I got busy and vacuumed and cleaned the house, had the locks changed, then went out to dinner to celebrate.

I stayed 10 years in San Diego, running Nordic Refrigeration and A/C until I retired in 87. Another chapter will cover that era.

CHAPTER 13

MY TENURE IN SAN DIEGO

*A*fter getting rid of Betty, I stayed in San Diego for the next 10 years.

Since they don't have any good trout fishing, elk hunting etc in Southern California I figured the best place to go for recreation was the ocean. Betty had been cleared out of the house so Dean and I thought the best thing to do was settle down see what we could do in this town. Earl Brooks was an old friend whom I had met when we lived in L.A. while I had worked for Lockheed. California Electric Works was looking for a General Manager for their various service departments, which consisted of an Electrical Service Department, A Pump Department, Sales Department, Onan Generator Dept. and another which I don't remember after 40 years.

The largest burr under my saddle was the fact that the Chairman of the Board had a son-in-law named Carl whom I was to train to take over my job down the line. Carl came in there with hair down to his shoulders, a full beard and looked to me like a miscarriage that lived and had been a drummer in a rock band. His tie to the Board Chairman was that he got his daughter pregnant and he was trying to make the best of a bad situation by trying to train this bum. Carl did cut his hair and shave but left his mustache on which was fine by me. I put him in charge of the electrical in house shop but any job I ever assigned to him he did not do well.

Onan wanted our company to have their distributor-ship in a separate building. We owned vacant ground right across the street and I wanted the Chairman to put up a concrete block building to house it. No Way.. Later I wanted to mount Onan generators on trailers and rent them out. No Way.

Our electrical warehouse was not secure and the service men came in and loaded their trucks with supplies without security or being inventoried by the warehouse foreman. We only had one man to monitor that so he could no way do that. We were running 24 to 28 trucks. I set traps and found some of the men were doing all sorts of work on week-ends and the cash went into their pockets. I wanted to fence off the warehouse and add more personnel to check out supplies. I wanted the service men to load their trucks after 5:00 or call in their orders during the day and then what went out could be monitored by the invoices they wrote and run through our computer.

After one year Carl did nothing to learn his job, The Onan shop did not get built, the generators did not get built and many other things. The Chairman, Norm Ferguson and I parted company.

I still had one truck left over from my Anaconda business so I ran an ad in the San Diego Tribune for 30 days and I did a lot of foot work dropping off business cards. I didn't get much from that but what I did, my customers liked my work and word got around, even in a big city like San Diego. I eventually was running four trucks and I never got larger than that. Just try hiring a qualified craftsman today and I would say it is the same as it was then. Run an ad and they come into your shop and tell you how many years experience they have and how great they are. I gave them a 20 question test of just the most basic elements on refrigeration, air conditioning and electrical theory, 75 percent failed the test. Most didn't even get 50 percent right. I also had men moonlighting on weekends and the parts they used didn't match what was on their billed invoices. Some tried changing parts that were not defective to make their paper look good. Those men came and were gone in short order. I still did well in that business. I installed and serviced a lot of those business's in 1980 and most stayed with me till I sold out in 1988. If a customer called me at 10:00 PM at night with a major problem, I or one of my men went to work. I also held the LaValencia Hotel account once I got it and they never let another contractor in there.

I once hired a bookkeeper through an agency and specified that she must be bonded. Sure, they sent out a Negro girl so I thought this would be fine I have no problem with that. So before they got the paper work finished to get her bonded, she took a check out of the back of the book, went down to the Ford agency and bought a new truck. It took about three days for me to find out what had happened. She was fired on the spot and I went to the Mission Valley Ford dealer and took a look at the check she wrote and it was a lousy forgery. I lit into the Manager and then of course my bank had tipped me off so I didn't lose anything but if sure was frustrating. I notified the Police, but they could care less. The dealer didn't care because he had run it through the Ford Credit Union that carried mortgages on new sales. Since they don't have any good trout fishing, elk hunting etc in Southern California I figured the best place to go for recreation was the ocean.

After I got rid of Betty Boops, I checked around and found that they had a singles sailing club that had just started called Polaris Sailing Club. They met every Tuesday at one of the hotels out in Pacific Beach and if you wanted to learn how to sail, just sign a roster and they would assign you to go out on the next Saturday or Sunday with someone who owned a boat, no charge. It was a very nice club and they held dances, had beach parties where we had raft-ups of several boats in Mission Bay and would have a volley ball net set up on the beach, a BBQ etc. It was a truly nice club. At times they would have parties at some-ones house, usually with a meal or BBQ, dance, etc. In fact I held several at my house. I had a nice den on the lower level with a bar, juke box and pool table.

It was at this time that I learned how to sail and got very good at it. I remember once when a German lady in the club owned a boat and asked me to teach her more about sailing. We went out into the ocean with a good breeze blowing and in order not to have to tack I held a course and with the wind at about a 90 degree angle and the boat healed over till the sails were really laying low. She really got nervous but I tried to assure her that the boat would not capsize because the more the boat healed over the wind would wash off the top of the sails. Anyway I obeyed her and changed course a bit.

After a few months I had a small boat on D dock at Mission Bay and this large yacht pulled in and had to tie up on the end tie because it was too large to use a slip. The Captain was Joe Meshade and we got acquainted with him and before long he had to take the boat out and invited some of us to handle lines for him. After that the owner came into town one weekend and I went out with Joe to handle lines and got to meet Dick and Lolita Kolar. They were very friendly people and we became friends.

During this time I helped Joe do some maintenance in the engine room and the builder of the boat had made some errors and I tried to help Joe on weekends. One being that they had used a used forklift engine to run the generator and the generator was too small to carry the entire load. Since I still had connections from California Electric I was able to buy a new generator at close out prices. The one that was on it was about a four KW unit which would not carry all the load. I figured we needed a seven KW unit but none was available at a reasonable price. I found a 16 KW for $900 which was less than half price and since it was oversized it didn't matter because the engine would pull all the KW we would need. We had to have a heavier frame to support the generator and Joe had that built. When all was ready five of our friends showed up and we hauled it aboard. I was nervous because to get it on the swim deck and in the gate to the fantail was a difficult task. We were sweating it out for fear that we would drop it in the ocean. Then getting it through the main salon and down into the engine room was no easy task but we did it. In the coming week Joe hooked up the wiring.

Joe was a nice guy but he lived on the boat and he smoked three packs a day of cigarettes. It wasn't too long after this that the owner Mr. Kolar called Renee and asked if I would be interested in skippering his boat. Joe would never let anyone at the helm but I had been running other smaller boats. When Renee told me of Dick's phone call, I jumped at the idea. Dick came over to San Diego and with a certified Captain we took the boat out. We went out into the bay and brought it back and docked it three times. Wally told Dick that this guy won't have any problem, so I became Mr Kolars' Captain of his 58 foot boat. While with the Polaris Club I had taken two or three Coast Guard courses so I wasn't a complete dummy.

After I took over, Renee, a Polaris member came to help me Scrub down the entire interior of Cigarette smoke stains. Everything was yellow and smelled terrible.

During the next months Dick and Lolita and friends came over and it was enjoyable. Many times after a day out we would swing by Anthony's Harbor restaurant and enjoy a dinner. Another favorite was Bali Hai which had a nice place to dock and they always had a good show and fine meals. One time after dinner, Lolita was practicing the stick dance with the Hawaii dancers and she missed a few times and ended up with some ankle bruises. Sometimes we would just stay tied up to their dock all night and go home in the morning.

Tom Ham's Light House was also good but it was right on the bay and boats going by could create a problem. One time we were going to dock there and we had Lolita, Margarita and a couple of guys who would like to have been one of her boyfriends. The dock had some steel pilings on the edge of the dock which required extra care in docking. I pulled into the dock and everyone got off I asked the guys to handle lines which was a joke. They got the stern line on but the muscle boy up front stood there like a dunce. An excursion boat went by too fast and created a wake. I yelled to the kid to push off the bow and he just stood there. The wake caused by the excursion boat caused a wake that raised our bow up and when it came down it hit the hull and put a thumb-nail size gouge in the gel coat. I was yelling while I was heading down from the bridge and I shoved the bow off to prevent further damage. I think I asked the kid if he was crippled or something because a kid could have held the boat off. We pulled the stern lines tighter to pull the boat back a couple of feet and all was OK. Thank God Margarita used her head when she was choosing who would be her husband. In my opinion she sure made a fine decision when she said yes to Mike Struckman.

Dick was in town in January one year when a storm was blowing into San Diego. He and I were on the boat and the small craft warning flag was up. He was wondering how the boat would handle in rough waters. I told him from what I knew of his boat there wouldn't be any problem. We decided to take it out, so we cast off the lines and headed out. We listened to the weather reports and they recommended all small craft to stay off the ocean as they said 12 foot waves were present with winds of 20 Knots. As we went past the Coast Guard station they raised the gale warning flag but we proceeded on out. When we got past the kelp beds we quartered the waves, no problem, then headed straight into the waves, not even any spray over the bow. We then got another weather report 18 foot waves were present. We then did get some spray over the bow but it rode the waves out beautifully. I even put the boat in a trough and with the way the keel was built on this boat it still did not have a severe roll. Satisfied with our sea test we headed in, tied up and had a toast to our test.

This boat had an excellent exterior design which the Henwoods bragged about their 18 year old son Mark who designed it. He may have done a good job on the exterior design but the interior was an abortion. The master suite had about a five and one half foot bed and to get by them to the head you had approximately 12 inches. Dick had bunk beds installed crosswise to accommodate a six foot person.

In the engine room they had an automotive type compressor, belt driven to furnish refrigeration for the beer cooler, refrigerator and freezer.

This would be fine while you are at sea but when you are at dock you would have to run the generator to have any refrigeration. Also, they used two inch Styrofoam insulation for the units and this was insufficient so keep frost from coming through. The finished wood paneling would have a layer of frost coming through into the galley.

I removed all the units, had the metal housings cut down about two inches to allow for more insulation. I then had them foamed in with polyurethane which would guarantee no frost bleed-through. I also installed separate quality temperature controls to make sure they were regulated properly. In the engine room, I removed the automotive air conditioner compressor from the generator and discarded that. In place of that I installed a two horse-power 110 volt compressor on the bench close to the galley units.

When all of this was going on I thought to myself, "If Dick Kolar could see his yacht right now he would fire me". That galley was a mess.

The end result was that when you are at sea you would have to run the generator anyway for refrigeration but when you are in dock and plugged into dock power you had free electric anyway.

Another big error in design was in the bilge area in the front 20 feet of the boat. This area was separated from the engine room by a water tight bulkhead. No bilge pump and the only access was through the floor in the forward bow area. They also had installed the front hot water heater up there and it had a flaw in that it would over heat and the hot water ran into the forward bilge area. No one including me had checked this as we should have until the bow was noted one day riding a little low sitting at the dock. I had to jury-rig a hose to go in there and pump it out.

Another major flaw in my opinion was the steel plate fastened mid ship under the bottom of the hull. This was anchored on the front edge and tapered down to about four inches at the rear. Through the hull was six exhaust pipes from the engines and the exhaust created an air foil under the ship which gave it a tremendous fuel savings.

This was a fine idea but the builder only anchored the steel plate with screws which were nowhere strong enough to hold this. When Dick sold the boat, the back edge of this plate was a angling ready to fall off. The son of the builder did repair that. However it should have been anchored most likely with good through-hull fittings.

One day I was loafing and had visited with John DeLori (I think that was his name) in his sales office on the dock. I mentioned some of the faults to him and my end remark was, "It's inconceivable that an 18 year old kid could design a boat like this, but again, when I see all the faults in this boat maybe it was designed by an 18 year old kid". I didn't know that he was a good friend of the builder and he related everything I had said. I was enemy numero-uno.

The last month that I skippered the boat Lolita and five or six of her girl friends came over and I took off a lot of time to take them out almost every day. One lady insisted on wearing high heels 1and the winding staircase going up to the bridge and the handrails did get scratched but for the most part washing down would have sufficed. They convinced Dick that the interior of the boat would have to be sanded and varnished from bow to stern. I think they got to Dick for about 10 grand. Also I was enemy # uno.

Twenty some years later I still love Dick and Lolita and while writing this Carol & I are in his mountain home in Flagstaff a small little log shack of 6000 Sq. ft.

Wife 6, Carol

I had lived in San Diego now for about eight years and now had plenty of experience on the open seas. Someone one suggested that since I also liked bicycle riding that I should show up on Sunday morning at the County offices parking lot at 9:00 Am. I loaded my bike into the back of my pickup the following Sunday and went there. Several groups showed up and the younger ones were in one group etc.

I picked the one with mostly seniors in it. I had an old Huffy and I later learned that I better get something that is a little easier peddling. I finally bought a Schwin bike and it was good but very heavy and by the time we made the 20 to 25 mile ride I was tired. One weekend we trucked all our bikes to San Clemente and then rode the 60 miles back to San Diego. I was in good shape by then but I was still very tired by the time we got back. I had accepted the position of sweeper, carrying a small American Flag during all these rides and on the way back we were coming up Torry Pines hill at La Jolla when we passed a young girl who was resting. She inquired as to what group we were with. I yelled back that we were the Senior Olympics Training Team. She said "wow" and we kept going. We got a little chuckle out of that one.

We usually had 15 to 25 people in our group and the purpose of the Sweeper on the tail end was to help anyone who had a flat or other problems. We would also send a speeder to the front end to stop the leader. We all liked to stay in a group and never leave anyone stranded out there. Bill Walsh was the leader and our whole group became a close knit bunch of friends.

One of the ladies there always came with Joe Kase and for a long time I thought they were married. At our mid-point coffee break one day something came up just right and I made the remark to Joe; "you better keep an eye on your wife or someone will steal her". Joe said, oh we're not married we're just friends and ride down here together. Later I found out that they had been skating partners in the La Jolla Figure Skating Club for years. After a few more weeks I noticed this cute doll was not riding up with the front group but was just ahead of the sweeper in back. When we got back from our ride sometime later I mentioned that I wasn't tired yet and asked if anyone wanted to join me and go to San Diego Sea Food on Harbor Island for lunch. She was the only one that wanted to go so off we went. She mentioned that she was getting a divorce from her husband. I sold my business later and mentioned that I was going to Phoenix and she wanted to ride down and visit her mother who lived there.

That was the first time that I had gone anywhere with Carol so one morning I picked her up and off we went. We stopped at a Café in El Cajon and had breakfast. We both ate pancakes and link sausage. I apparently got some bad sausage because before we got to El Centro I had to rush to make the toilet in the restaurant. Thirty miles farther I just barely made the rest stop and the same at Yuma. This went on till we were on the North bound highway #85 and I couldn't find a rest stop so I pulled over and headed for some brush by a culvert. I didn't make it and that is where I left my shorts. When I returned to the car, I got a towel out of the trunk and put it on my seat. I apologized to Carol and said we would have to ride with the windows down the rest of the way.

It was dark when we got to Anitas house, she is Dick Kolar's office manager and I was going to stay at his house that night. She came out to the car to make sure who she was giving the house key to. She then gave it to Carol and we proceeded on to Saguaro Drive to Dick's house. When I got into the house I headed straight for the laundry room, emptied my pockets, stripped all clothing, put them in the washer and went to the shower. Carol found me a robe in a closet and I put that on. By now I was empty and I told her where the bar was and had her mix us a scotch and soda. We drank those and I was over my diarrhea. One good thing about my body, I don't get a lot of belly pain with food poisoning, it will defecate the poisons from my body and get rid of it. Many people get intense pain and have to go to the hospital emergency room. I went to a small store and bought some food and we ate. I told her she could pick a bed and that we would have to stay there for the night. Dick's house was 5100 square feet so there was plenty of room.

Carol was so understanding on the whole trip and I took her to her mother's place the following day. I figured most women would say to themselves, never again with that guy.

I stayed at Dicks for four days and did some minor electrical detail work on the house before Carol & I headed back to San Diego. Dick had his house up for sale so I did some detail eye-wash work to make it look better.

My business had been sold shortly after that, Dick and I had developed a pretty close friendship while I was Captain of his yacht. I had been to his ranch in Colorado several times and he told me if I wanted a place to retire he would give me a one acre lot on his ranch on which to build my retirement log cabin. I took him up on that deal. The ranch was 541 acres located seven miles up the canyon from Lake George and about a mile from the 11 Mile Reservoir. It was a beautiful site and was surrounded by forest service land on three sides. Dick and Lolita let me live in their house up there while I was building my cabin.

In the meantime I was spending time back in San Diego selling my house and cleaning up loose ends and spending some time with Carol. She liked the idea of my log cabin and thought she would love to live in a place like that. In the first summer I rented a fifth wheel trailer to live in so that Dick and Lolita would have their house. Carol flew up and at that time I only had the basement forms up ready to pour concrete. I sat her down and laid out my rules "JOHN WAYNE STYLE", Any woman that wants to live with me up there has to accept the fact that this is where I am going to retire and live out my life; HA! famous last words. When she saw the plans she was ecstatic. All the logs were to be 12 inch diameter, milled, with a Swedish cope cut.

The living room was to be 34 x 27 feet, the office 10 X 17 feet, master bedroom 17 X 19 feet, kitchen 12 X 15 feet, and the master bath was split, a four x six foot marble Jacuzzi tub, a large shower at the end of the tub and the toilet room was separate with a toilet, bidet, urinal and a vanity at one end. Looking back, the only mistake I made was in making the kitchen too small. The fireplace sat in the center of the south wall and was the showpiece of the Great Room. I had imported eight barrels of geodes from Brazil and the entire front of the fireplace was set with half inch thick polished geodes and three petrified polished tree slabs from Holbrook, Arizona. Down stairs were 2 extra bedrooms, a bath and sewing room for Carol, plus a 12 X 27 foot rec room.

My log cabin retirement house had gotten away from me, it ended up being 3700 square feet and a 26 X 36 foot garage. Two to a dozen cars would drive by every weekend to view my progress and upon completion people kept asking if we would have an open house. In June of 89 I rented a budget truck and moved Carol up and on December 19th we held the open house. In that six months, due to the fact that Ed Diltz ripped me off and didn't finish the kitchen cabinets after he had conned me into paying him in full, I finally had to take him to court to get my cabinets. During this time she cooked on a hot plate and a microwave oven and washed dishes in the bathroom sink. But by the open house date we had it all finished upstairs and Carol, without neighbors help, cooked a 21 pound turkey, a ham and loads of other food and her big dining table was loaded from one end to the other. The open bar was set up in the kitchen and only two people made a pig of themselves on that. Now would you believe this? That afternoon a big blizzard blew in and dropped about six inches of snow. We thought with a storm like that, no one would come, surprise, 67 people showed up and it was a total success.

Shortly after that we got a call from Arizona from Carol's mother that Cleet had cancer and wanted us kids to come down and help her take care of him. We wanted her to rent us an apartment or something so we would have a place to stay when we got there. She said during the winters, there is nothing available without paying a fortune for it. She suggested we buy a used motor home in Colorado to live in while we are there. It ended up that we bought a 77 class A Cruise-Aire from a minister in Denver for $9,000. We headed south within a few days and when we got to I-40 in New Mexico we found that it was closed near Flagstaff. I went all the way to the southern part of the state and came up through Tucson to Phoenix and then into Mesa where her mother lived at Sun Life Park in Mesa. We found a parking spot in Mesa Regal and stayed there the winter.

Poor Cleet had Melanoma cancer and died on February ninth of 1990. Carol and I got married in January of that year and Cleet was able to see some pictures. We stayed until March fifth and then headed back to Lake George in Colorado. I then sold the Cruise Aire for $500 more than I paid for it.

The reason Carol and I didn't marry sooner was because of our government's greediness for money. Each of us had a house to sell and if we were married, only one of us could receive the $125,000 tax deduction on selling our home.

In June of that year, Carol's mother had some tests and they found a spot on her lung. In Denver they wanted to do a biopsy and they were trying to go through the bulk of the breast to get into the lung. She was so angry; she stopped them and said she would go to the Mayo Clinic in Scottsdale. The earliest appointment she could get was for September so she had Carol drive her down because she was getting quite a bit of pain. As soon as Carol got back we loaded our Prowler 35 foot fifth wheel trailer up that Carol had bought in Sand Diego and headed for Mesa, Arizona to take care of her Mother.

She died December tenth and we stayed until April of the following year. When we got back to our new log home in Lake George, I told Carol we could now get the estate cleared up and we could settle down for our retirement in Colorado. Her retort was, "I'm not living up here in the winter, I like Arizona". So it ended up that we have been migrating back to Mesa every year since. We bought a little Park Model and set it on a lot in Mesa Regal and the annual rent was $1200 a year. That wasn't bad considering it only cost us $200 a month for the lot lease for the six months that we were there. They had three swimming pools, tennis courts, volley ball courts, library, pool room, card rooms, and a lot more that are too numerous to itemize. In about 1993 five of us guys got together and started a Computer Club. At first we would take Jim Wilts computer down to a classroom every Thursday and he taught us about Dos and the word processor. As we learned those we taught them to the new students and as we got new programs like Parsons Technology, we taught others about that. By the year 2000 they had 17 computers in the class room all on line, and 425 senior members.

The Park sold several times and it was like the Utility companies, each new buyer had to make more profit. They raised the rent about $200 a year and by 1997 when we sold our park model and moved out the rent was about $2800 a year. We sold the unit and were fortunate we thought to recoup all the money we had invested in it.

In the meantime, back at the ranch in Colorado, we would find that during the summer we would take our trailer and tour the various parts of the U.S. and Canada. Carol wasn't all that happy living in the mountains of Colorado and since we were only living in that new home about three months out of a year, we decided to sell it. Nothing happens as is planned. Before we got married or even before I started the house, I laid it down JOHN WAYNE style. This is where I am going to retire and any woman that I marry better make up her mind right now, this is going to be my retirement cabin. Famous last words, that cabin turned into a 3700 square foot Lodge and we have had two additional homes since and the last one in Polson is now up for sale.

At about the same time Dick decided to sell the Ranch and a Doctor of Chiropractic bought it and he also liked our house so we sold it to him. We carried paper on it for him and between the profit on the initial sale and the interest coming in we made a nice profit.

Carol and I were tooling around one New Year's eve back in '96 and found an empty lot for sale in Mesa East, a senior park where you owned your own ground. We bought it for $30,000 and put an 1800 square foot manufactured home on it. Then I am one who hates to leave your equipment out in the weather, I built a 24 X 40 foot garage to house our RV and our truck plus a small workshop in the corner.

It is 2003 at this writing and it has been for Sale for two years and since it is one of the more expensive units in the park, it hasn't sold yet. It sold in 2003. After we sold the Colorado house we moved our base camp to Arizona. I didn't like that so I came to Montana in 2001 and bought a nice home just outside of Polson. Then I built a 24 X 42 feet garage and a side extension 14 X 30ft boat house. Carol wanted a boat if she was going to live by a lake so I found a 21 foot Sun Tracker pontoon boat with only about a 100 hrs. on it for $10,500 and it is very nice for this lake. It is great to fish off of and it will handle just about any weather that we might get on this lake. With a 90 HP Merc it also can get out and move. Flathead is 28 miles long and 15 miles wide at its widest point so it can give you a run for your money in rough weather.

We have two and two thirds acres here overlooking Flathead Lake. My reasoning was that when we get to old to RV back and forth we needed some place where we could live year around and I thought it would not be too cold here and Carol would like it. WRONG. She is also unhappy here also.

Carol and I have now been married 21 years in 2009, it is now 2008 and things have come to pass. Carol has had 5 surgeries and has slowed down considerably. Last December of 06 I had spinal surgery, in May I had Knee surgery, two days later I had a stroke, October I had a hernia operation. In December of '08 I had a serious bowel infection, so things are winding down pretty fast. I did recover from the stroke quite well as far as my speech goes but I am not stable on my feet. When I got up that morning with the stroke Carol gave me the usual tests and I did pretty good till she made me write my name, I couldn't do it. She wouldn't even let me wait till I had a little breakfast; we went to the emergency room stat. Thanks to Carol for that.

In 2003 at 75, I rode a bicycle down Big Mountain trail in Whitefish and now look at me. Am I getting old?

Carol wants to go south again this winter and I don't, I used to have a name for wimp that did everything their wives wanted. We are going south in October of 2008.

Out to dinner Whitefish Cntry Club 2004